"Tim Challies is one of the finest young evangelical thinkers of our day. He combines keen insight with theological maturity and spiritual depth. *The Discipline of Spiritual Discernment* should help form the Christian character of a new generation of evangelicals. Indeed, we must hope so."

> —R. ALBERT MOHLER JR., president, The Southern Baptist
> Theological Seminiary

"The many fans Tim Challies has won through his highly regarded blog (Challies.com) will discover in this book the motivation that drives his incisive analysis of cultural events and trends—a keen respect for truth and a passionate commitment to biblical discernment."

> —NANCY PEARCEY, author, *Total Truth: Liberating Christianity from Its Cultural Captivity*

"If you want to be discerning, buy this book; if you read it, you will be! Tim Challies has written on a topic that is both important and rarely addressed. This book on discernment is simple, clear, well written and well illustrated, accurate, and even insightful. I read it all. I liked it all. I will recommend it often. Ten pithy chapters—read one a day for ten days, and I guess that you'll find yourself more discerning—or at least wanting to be."

> —MARK DEVER, pastor, Capitol Hill Baptist Church,
> Washington DC

"John Murray said, 'The difference between truth and error is not a chasm but a razor's edge.' Spurgeon said something like it too: 'Discernment is not a matter of simply telling the difference between what is right and wrong; rather, it is the difference between right and almost right.' Both these giants emphasized the vital quality (and difficulty) of discernment. Unfortunately, in our time, even among Christians, discernment is long in demand and short in supply. This is but one reason I'm so delighted to commend to you *The Discipline of Spiritual Discernment*. Tim reminds us that the Bible constantly commands us to cultivate discernment, but he doesn't stop there. He tells us how."

> —LIGON DUNCAN, senior minister, First Presbyterian Church,
> Jackson, Mississippi

"The path to most biblical graces is bordered with hazards on both sides of the way. With the subject of this book—discernment—one can fall into the ditch of careless naivetè on the left or wander into the dark woods of a critical spirit on the right. Tim Challies carefully guides his reader between these dangers and on toward Christlike discernment. I've simply never read a more thorough, practical, and biblically sound treatment of this subject. Anyone wanting to study biblical discernment should not miss this book."

—DON WHITNEY, associate professor of biblical spirituality; senior associate dean at The Southern Baptist Theological Seminary

FOREWORD BY **JOHN MacARTHUR**

the **DISCIPLINE**
of **SPIRITUAL**
DISCERNMENT

tim challies

CROSSWAY BOOKS
WHEATON, ILLINOIS

Library of Congress Cataloging-in-Publication Data
Challies, Tim, 1976–
   The discipline of spiritual discernment / Tim Challies.
     p. cm.
   Includes bibliographical references and indes.
   ISBN 978-1-58134-909-2 (tpb)
    1. Discernment (Christian theology). I. Title.
BV45209.5.C427   2007
248.2—dc22   2007032348

VP		18	17	16	15	14	13	12	11		10	09	08
15	14	13	12	11	10	9	8	7	6	5	4	3	

To

Aileen,

whom I love second only
to the One who brought us together.

CONTENTS

FOREWORD

TODAY'S EVANGELICALS ARE confronted with a multitude of new perspectives, emerging trends, and evangelical fads—all claiming to be more biblical or more effective than the ideas they seek to overthrow. With such a broad patchwork of competing ideas all clamoring for mainstream acceptance, how can the average person in the pew be expected to know what is truly sound, safe, and biblical? In a world where everything seems colored in shades of gray, how can Christians develop the discipline of discernment?

Tim Challies is uniquely qualified to write on the subject. I don't know of a more reliable or more prolific commentator on the contemporary evangelical scene. His weblog is a favorite stop for thousands of Christian readers every day. His book reviews and his comments on evangelical trends are consistently evenhanded, thorough yet succinct, and full of perceptive insights. Tim obviously values clarity and biblical accuracy—and those qualities all come through in this excellent work as well. *The Discipline of Spiritual Discernment* is a truly important work—one that should be required reading not only for church leaders, but for all sober-minded laypeople as well.

—JOHN MACARTHUR, pastor-teacher,
Grace Community Church,
Sun Valley, California

INTRODUCTION

EARLY ONE MORNING, in the spring of 1945, Ida Weisenbacher, a twenty-one-year-old Austrian farm girl, was woken from her sleep by a loud banging at the door. Through tired eyes she glimpsed a Nazi officer standing outside her house. "Get up immediately," he demanded. "Hitch up the horse and wagon; we need you." Obediently, and now wide awake, Ida quickly hitched her horse to the wagon and waited while soldiers hurriedly loaded it with large wooden crates. Each crate was identical and unmarked, save for a label with bold-painted letters and numbers. Ida did not dare to ask what the crates contained. There were too many of these mysterious boxes to fit a single load, so when the wagon was full, the officer barked that she was to drive to the shores of nearby Lake Toplitz. She quickly realized why the German army had requisitioned her wagon: the track to the lake was too rugged for a truck to pass. Only a horse-drawn wagon could make the journey.

She made the brief trip three times. As she arrived with the final load, she saw that a group of soldiers had paddled into the midst of Toplitz and were dropping the crates into the depths of the lake. It would be fifty-five years before this German secret was uncovered.

There are few places on earth better equipped to conceal a secret. Located within a dense forest and surrounded by the tall mountains of Austria, Lake Toplitz is small—only a mile long. But what the lake lacks in size, it makes up for in depth, for the bottom is some 350 feet below the surface. Isolated, surrounded by rugged, inhospitable terrain and filled with nearly freezing waters, Toplitz may as well be the moon. And in fact, men would uncover the secrets of the moon long before they would uncover the secrets of Toplitz.

It was 1945 and the world was at war. Adolf Hitler, the man responsible for beginning the conflict, was dead, having taken his own life in his mountain fortress. A few die-hard Nazis held out some hope that Germany's new leader could somehow reverse the tide; most knew it was far too late. The armies of the United States and Great Britain were closing in from the west, and hordes of Russian soldiers were approaching from the east. It was now inevitable that as she had done only three decades earlier, Germany would be forced to surrender to her foes. Yet through her conquests, Germany had amassed an incredible wealth of treasure, much of which was stolen from men and women who had been put to death in the infamous concentration camps. As the Allied armies approached Germany, much of this treasure—gold and silver, paintings and ornaments—was hidden away in mountain caves. Those who knew of Toplitz supposed that some of Hitler's treasure was hidden away in the depths of the lake.

In 1999, a team of explorers led by the CBS news program *60 Minutes II* journeyed to Lake Toplitz to attempt to recover the crates they learned had been hidden there. *60 Minutes II* retained the services of Oceaneering, a company specializing in undersea exploration. Oceaneering, which had been responsible for recovering the wreckage of the Space Shuttle Challenger and T.W.A. Flight 800, decided to make use of The Phantom, a deep-diving robot tethered to an operator who controls it from the surface. For three weeks, and for nearly ten hours a day, the crew scoured the bottom of the lake but were unable to locate the boxes. And then at last they found something—a small piece of wood that looked as if it may have once been a portion of a crate. They knew they were near to their treasure. But as The Phantom brought this plank to the surface, it slipped from the vessel's grasp and sank out of sight.

Oceaneering refused to be discouraged and called for WASP, their high-tech, one-man submersible. A WASP operator, Ken Tyler, descended some 200 feet to the debris field and found vast quantities of paper that had been lying undisturbed for fifty-five years. "It's very, very fragile. It's falling to bits," he reported from the lake's floor. When the paper was moved, it quickly disintegrated into pulp.

Gingerly, Tyler finally secured a bundle of the paper and carefully brought it to the surface. As this paper broke the surface of the water, it brought an end to one of Hitler's greatest secrets. Printed on the paper were the words, "Bank of England." The crates that were dropped into Lake Toplitz, the crates Ida Weisenbacher had carried to the edge of the lake so many years before, had been filled with hundreds of millions of pounds in counterfeit British currency.

Adolf Burger was one of the men responsible for creating these banknotes. A printer by trade, and a Jewish native of Czechoslovakia, he was arrested by the Germans on August 10, 1942, and soon separated from his wife, whom he had married only weeks earlier. Like so many millions of Jews before and after them, Burger and his wife were packed into a livestock train and taken to Auschwitz, expecting to be quickly put to death. At the camp Burger was torn from his wife, whom he would never see again. After some time in custody he was ordered to appear before the camp commandant. When he did so, he was notified, to his amazement, that he would be leaving the next day and would be taken to Berlin where his services were urgently needed. He soon found himself in a secure camp at Sauchsenhausen in the company of dozens of other craftsmen—printers, bookbinders, engravers—who had likewise been selected from death camps and told of a secret project. Code-named Operation Bernard, this brilliant project was part of a Nazi plot to produce a vast quantity of counterfeit British currency. This cash, when released into circulation in Great Britain, would cause widespread economic panic, undermine the value of the British pound, destroy her economy, and perhaps even drive the nation to its knees.

In general counterfeiters do the least work possible in creating phony money. The majority of forgeries reflect only as much effort as is necessary to create a bill that can pass a cursory inspection. Because of this, most counterfeit currency is easily detected and confiscated before it can enter circulation. The Bernard bills, though, were to be masterpieces that could fool even a trained expert. John Keyworth of the Bank of England said that counterfeiters consistently face two problems. The first is to create a convincing forgery.

But by using some of the world's finest craftsmen and supplying these men with the most modern tools and machinery, the Germans solved this problem.

The second difficulty is in distributing the currency. Once a bill leaves the hands of its creator, the plan succeeds, for the money is then in circulation. Because most counterfeit bills are of inferior quality and are produced in small amounts, they are often passed in bars or nightclubs and other locations where they are difficult to adequately examine. But the Germans intended to release hundreds of millions of pounds, far more than could be passed discreetly in safe locations. Relying on the predictability of human nature, they made a plan to release the money from bombers flying over major British cities. They knew that many people would collect this money and hand it to the proper authorities. But they knew that far more would horde and distribute the money despite knowing it to be counterfeit. Money falling from the sky would be too great a temptation. Once the bills were in circulation, it would be difficult for even experts to know genuine from counterfeit; amateurs would have no hope.

Had the German plan succeeded, millions of citizens, banks, and shops would have been fooled into accepting this worthless money. Such a massive influx of counterfeit currency could prove fatal to a nation's economy. Shops might refuse to sell their goods, fearing that money they received for their wares would prove worthless. Banks might refuse to accept or distribute cash. Without currency, goods would not exchange hands. Panic and chaos would ensue. The economy of even a great nation could be devastated by such a devious plan.

For two years, Burger and the rest of the team labored to produce near-perfect banknotes. They were supplied with the finest craftsmen and the latest printing equipment. The operation eventually produced today's equivalent of 4.5 billion dollars in banknotes that were nearly indiscernible from the originals. When they had mastered British currency and had produced it in massive quantities, the team began to perfect a copy of the American hundred-dollar bill. They were soon prepared to produce a daily output of one million dollars in phony bills. But then, with the Russian army only a few hundred kilometers from Berlin, the Germans were suddenly ordered to dismantle the machinery and to abandon the project. Before Burger was returned to a concentration camp, he was ordered to pack the banknotes into large wooden crates, crates that were soon being driven on the back of a wagon to the shores of Lake Toplitz.

Though some quantity of the Operation Bernard banknotes entered into circulation—most of it used to pay German spies and secret agents—the Germans never acted on their plan to inundate England with this counterfeit currency. History has failed to record a definitive answer as to why they did not do this. It may have been one of the many providences of the war, for Operation Bernard, if carried to its planned conclusion, could have changed the course of World War II. Counterfeit currency could have changed the world.[1]

While this is not a book about counterfeit currency, it deals with a topic that is surprisingly similar, though with consequences far more serious. As you no doubt surmised from its title, this is a book about discernment—about the skill of thinking biblically about life. To be more precise, it is a book about a particular kind of discernment: *spiritual* discernment. In this book I hope to show that discernment is a discipline, and like other disciplines such as prayer and reading the Bible, it is one that all Christians should seek to practice and should seek to practice deliberately. If we are to be a people who show our love for the Lord by faithfully serving him, it is a discipline we *must* practice.

This book is written for the general reader who wishes to understand discernment and to understand what the Bible teaches us about discernment, and who wishes to equip himself in this discipline. It is not written primarily for people with theological training, though I trust they, too, can benefit from it. Rather, it is written for you and for me—average Christians living in a culture

---

[1]Information was drawn from various articles, including http://www.cbsnews.com/stories/2000/11/21/ 60II/main251320.shtml; http://www.channel4.com/community/showcards/G/Great_Nazi_Cash_ Swindle.html; and http://www.unmuseum.org/nazigold.htm. The episode of *60 Minutes II* is available for purchase from the CBS web site.

and in a church where it so often seems that anything goes. It is written for those who look at much of what is said and done in the name of Jesus and ask themselves, "How can this be right?" It is written for all those who believe that it is the duty of every Christian to *think* biblically about all areas of life so that they might *act* biblically in all areas of life.

I have premised this book on my belief that there are many Christians who wish to grow in discernment, and who are eager to receive Bible-based teaching on this topic. There are none who know all there is to know about discernment. There are none who are unable to grow in this area. And yet there is very little teaching on this topic. My research led me to only a handful of books dealing with the subject, and few of those titles remain in print.

I do not intend to do the work of discernment for you. There are many books, web sites, and ministries that claim to teach discernment but do so by simply listing all the things you must do and the things you must not do. This book approaches the subject differently and is the result of my studies in Scripture to find the tools of discernment that God provides to us in his Word. And so I will not present a list of ministries you should avoid or endorse, authors whose books you should burn or buy, and music you should not listen to or that you should immediately download to your MP3 player. Rather, I hope to teach biblical wisdom on how you and I can become more discerning. I will present to you the wisdom of the Bible as it teaches us how we can become men and women of discernment. I will present principles you can use as you walk this life distinguishing between what is truth and what is error, what is right and what is wrong.

It is my hope and prayer that this book will stir you and me and others to answer the call for discernment so that together we may learn to discern truth from error, good from bad, better from best. I trust that God will equip us to think biblically about life so that we may bring him all glory, praise, and honor.

Before we begin our study, I would like to provide a brief outline of the book to help you understand how we will progress in our understanding and application of discernment.

Chapter 1 provides a call to discernment by showing both the benefits of acquiring discernment and the cost of ignoring it. The second chapter discusses the challenge of discernment, looking at three types of influences that make discernment a particular challenge in our day and in our culture. Not until the third chapter is the term *discernment* defined. While this may seem strange, I encourage you to bear with me—you'll soon understand the logic in waiting.

Chapter 4 presents the heart of discernment and the right of the Christian to judge between what is right and wrong and what is true and false. In chapters 5 and 6 we look at the two broad areas of life that require us to exercise discernment: knowing the truth and discerning the will of God for our lives.

The seventh chapter looks at discernment as a gift of the Spirit, and chapter 8 presents the potential dangers inherent in a distorted understanding of discernment. Chapter 9 examines the commitments, context, character, and confirmation of discernment. The tenth and final chapter provides a framework for discernment, leading the reader through the process of discernment in a step-by-step format. We will then wrap things up, praying and trusting that God will equip us to be Christians who value and practice the discipline of discernment. The appendix, containing a list of valuable resources on discernment, may prove beneficial to those interested in studying this topic further.

You will no doubt note that I refer to and quote the Bible many times throughout this book. I do so, simply because I have nothing to offer but what Scripture says. I have certainly not mastered the discipline of discernment and have written this book as much for my benefit as for yours. I have approached this book with what I hope is a spirit of humility, asking God to direct my mind and to lead me to the portions of Scripture that are most relevant to this study. I believe he has been gracious in doing so, and I trust that you will benefit as much from reading this study as I have from writing it. So please do not glance fleetingly at the passages I reproduce in the text, and especially those at the beginning of chapters. Rather, read them slowly and meditatively, letting them penetrate your soul. I have not inserted verses of Scripture simply to prove my case; rather, these verses *are* my case. If you are to remember anything from this book, let it be not my words, but the words of the Bible.

We will begin our study with a call to discernment.

chapter one

a CALL to DISCERNMENT

*By the Holy Spirit who dwells within us, guard the
good deposit entrusted to you.*

2 TIMOTHY 1:14

IT MUST BE TERRIFYING to be the son of a king and to be heir
to a throne. A prince always lives with the knowledge that, at some
point, his father will die, and he will have to step in as successor.
He will have to assume the throne of his father and rule the nation,
and an entire country will depend on his wisdom and his ability. A
foolish prince might imagine this to be a simple task and might rel-
ish the power and glory that will be his. A wise prince will tremble,
knowing his inadequacy for the task.

Just such a man is described in the Bible. Following the great
King David, whom God describes in Acts as "a man after my
heart" (Acts 13:22), stood Solomon. Though he was already a
grown man when he became king, Solomon was wise and considered himself as little more than a child who was still dependent on a Father's wisdom. In the book of 1 Kings we learn that
while Solomon was at Gibeon to offer sacrifices to the Lord, God
appeared to him in a dream and said simply, "Ask what I shall
give you" (1 Kings 3:5). We are commonly taught that Solomon

asked the Lord for wisdom, and that God, being pleased with this request, instantaneously blessed him with a great outpouring of this gift. But in Solomon's words we see that he requests more than wisdom: he requests discernment. Solomon's humble prayer is recorded for us in 1 Kings 3:6–9:

> "You have shown great and steadfast love to your servant David my father, because he walked before you in faithfulness, in righteousness, and in uprightness of heart toward you. And you have kept for him this great and steadfast love and have given him a son to sit on his throne this day. And now, O LORD my God, you have made your servant king in place of David my father, although I am but a little child. I do not know how to go out or come in. And your servant is in the midst of your people whom you have chosen, a great people, too many to be numbered or counted for multitude. Give your servant therefore an understanding mind to govern your people, that I may discern between good and evil, for who is able to govern this your great people?"

I find this a deeply moving passage, for the cry of Solomon resounds in my heart. It is a cry born of deep humility and a profound sense of dependence upon God. "I am but a little child," he cries, "I do not know how to go out or come in." Ascending to the throne of his father, the renowned king, Solomon must have realized his frailty, his inadequacy.

Solomon's specific request is this: "Give your servant therefore an understanding mind to govern your people, that I may discern between good and evil" (1 Kings 3:9a). God reiterates and answers this request, saying to Solomon, "Because you have asked this, and have not asked for yourself long life or riches or the life of your enemies, but have asked for yourself understanding to discern what is right, behold, I now do according to your word" (1 Kings 3:11–12a). And here is what God gave Solomon: "Behold, I give you a wise and discerning mind, so that none like you has been before you and none like you shall arise after you" (1 Kings 3:12b).

Commenting on verse 9, Hebrew scholars Keil and Delitzsch

point out that the "understanding mind" Solomon requested was really a "hearing heart" or a "listening heart"—"a heart giving heed to the law and right of God."[1] Solomon was given wisdom, to be sure, but he was also given a hearing heart. He was given discernment such as no mere human has possessed before or since. We might even say that Solomon requested discernment, but because of the connectedness of wisdom and discernment, God gave him both what he requested and its important prerequisite. Solomon became both wise and discerning.

We can now read Solomon's psalm, written after the events of that night, a psalm in which he asks God's assistance in applying wisdom:

> Give the king your justice, O God,
>   and your righteousness to the royal son!
> May he judge your people with righteousness,
>   and your poor with justice!
> Let the mountains bear prosperity for the people,
>   and the hills, in righteousness!
> May he defend the cause of the poor of the people,
>   give deliverance to the children of the needy,
>   and crush the oppressor! (Ps. 72:1–4)

Unlike Solomon, I have not been called by God to govern a nation. But even in the humble ways God has called me to lead, I feel the desire of Solomon. Even when I look at my family and think of how I must lead my wife and teach my children, I feel like a little child, uncertain of what to do and how to act. So often I have called out to God for wisdom and for discernment. So often I have sought to be like Solomon. So often I have wanted to know that God is pleased with my requests.

God honored Solomon's request because he was pleased with what Solomon had asked. This teaches us that God values discernment and honors those who seek after it. In this chapter we will see the importance the Bible places on discernment by looking at both

---

[1] C. F. Keil and F. Delitzsch, *Commentary on the Old Testament: 1 and 2 Kings & 1 and 2 Chronicles* (Peabody, MA: Hendrickson, 1866), 31.

the curses that accompany a *lack* of discernment and the blessings that accompany the pursuit of discernment.

We see first that a lack of discernment must point to one of three unavoidable conclusions.

1) Lack of Discernment Is Proof of Spiritual Immaturity

In the closing verses of Hebrews 5, the author of this great letter warns his readers against apostasy, against straying from the faith:

> About this we have much to say, and it is hard to explain, since you have become dull of hearing. For though by this time you ought to be teachers, you need someone to teach you again the basic principles of the oracles of God. You need milk, not solid food, for everyone who lives on milk is unskilled in the word of righteousness, since he is a child. But solid food is for the mature, for those who have their powers of discernment trained by constant practice to distinguish good from evil. (Heb. 5:11–14)

The author of Hebrews has much he would like to tell the recipients of this letter. There is much knowledge he would like to impart to them, so many important things they need to learn. Unfortunately, what he wishes to communicate is "hard to explain" not because it is obscure or difficult to understand, but because the people have become "dull of hearing." They are not stupid people and are not intellectually inferior, unable to grasp such truths. The reason he cannot relay these important truths is not because of what these people are by nature, but of what they have *become*.[2] There is much the author would like to say, but he cannot and will not because of the spiritual immaturity of the people to whom he writes. They lack understanding, and they lack discernment.

The recipients of the letter to the Hebrews are not new Christians or recent converts, for the author says that by this time they ought to be teachers. This is not to say that they all ought to be ministers or preachers, but that they should all be sufficiently mature so they are able to understand and to teach others the basics of the faith. Sadly, though, they still have not understood the basics themselves.

---

[2]Phillip Hughes, *Hebrews* (Grand Rapids, MI: Eerdmans, 1977), 189.

They do not have the *childlike* faith Jesus so values but a *childish*, immature faith. In this way they are like so many Christians since then. Richard Phillips writes:

> The recipients of this letter were like many Christians today who think that theology is a waste of time. What difference does it make, people ask, whether God is a Trinity or not, whether Christ's righteousness comes by imputation or infusion, and whether regeneration comes before faith or after? What is important, they say, is that we get along with each other. Then they cite passages commending a *childlike* faith, as if that were the same thing as a *childish* faith, that is, one that is indifferent to or ignorant of the Word of God.[3]

We live in an age where too many who profess to be Christians rarely consider their spiritual maturity—an age when many consider spiritual immaturity a mark of authenticity, and when people associate doubt with humility and assurance with pride. Far too many people consider sound theology the mark of a person who is argumentative and proud. Far too many people are just like the audience to whom Hebrews is addressed. This letter draws a clear line connecting a lack of discernment with spiritual immaturity so that those who lack discernment are those who are spiritually immature. Scripture makes it plain: if you are not a person who exhibits and exercises discernment you are not a mature Christian.

My wife and I have been blessed with three children and often marvel that they have survived through infancy, for we have seen them put the most horrible and nauseating things in their mouths (things my editor will, wisely no doubt, not let me mention in this book!). Children have no understanding of what is good for them and will sample anything. Their mouths are constantly wide open, eager to taste and to eat anything that looks good to their untrained eyes. It is only with maturity that children learn what is truly good for them and what is not. Only with maturity will children learn that what *looks* good may not truly *be* good. Children need to learn to differentiate between what will hurt them and what will make them healthy.

---

[3] Richard Phillips, *Hebrews* (Phillipsburg, NJ: P&R, 2006), 177.

Eventually they learn to discriminate; they learn to discern. In the same way, mature Christians have learned to differentiate between what is pleasing to God and what is not, between what is consistent with Scripture and what is not. The Bible places great emphasis on spiritual maturity because, like children, immature believers are prone to sample anything. They are attracted to what looks good to their untrained eyes. Only as they grow in maturity are they able to differentiate between what pleases God and what does not. Because of this there can be no growth without discernment.

My wife and I have learned something else about children: children hate to be called children. Babies hate to be called babies. They don't like to be known as immature or childish, even when they clearly are. Every little boy wants to be a big boy. Every little girl wants to be a woman. God has somehow built into us a desire to mature. Every person wants to feel mature and grown up. When the author of Hebrews describes his readers as children he is not paying them a compliment, and he knows that they will be insulted. He hopes to show them their desperate condition and to impress upon them how serious their spiritual condition is. God demands and expects maturity, and maturity is inseparable from discernment. A Christian cannot have one without the other.

2) Lack of Discernment Is Proof of Backsliding

A lack of discernment is given as proof of spiritual immaturity, but this is not all. Those who are not discerning may also be those who are backsliding, whose faith is diminishing rather than increasing. "For though by this time you ought to be teachers, you need someone to teach you again the basic principles of the oracles of God. You need milk, not solid food, for everyone who lives on milk is unskilled in the word of righteousness, since he is a child" (Heb. 5:12–13). While the subjects of this letter should have been growing in their faith, progressing from milk to solid food, they were instead moving backwards, returning to baby food.

As children grow and mature, they begin to be able to eat and digest solid food. Most children are weaned quickly and encouraged to enjoy food more substantial than mere milk. Even while they are still tiny, children long for substantial food. It is good and natural that they desire that which will sustain them more than milk. We would not consider a child healthy who, at six years of age, still drinks only milk, for that child would be weak and sickly. The same is true in the spiritual realm. A person should pass quickly from spiritual milk to solid foods, from the basics to what is more advanced. A person should hunger to quickly learn and understand what is elementary and should soon long for what is more advanced. This is a sign of maturity and the mark of one who has been truly saved. On the other hand, a person who regresses from solid food to milk is a person who is desperately unhealthy, and who will soon wither away and perish.

The recipients of the letter to the Hebrews were regressing rather than progressing in their faith. There had been a time when they were able to hear what the author was so earnest to share with them now. Sadly, they are no longer at such a place. Their lack of discernment has caused them to lose ground. They are moving backwards rather than forwards. They are backslidden.

Solid food is a long way off from these people, for "solid food is for the mature, for those who have their powers of discernment trained by constant practice to distinguish good from evil" (Heb. 5:14). Until these people learn to practice discernment and to do so constantly, they will not be able to handle solid food. Until they practice discernment and learn to distinguish between what is good and what is evil, they will continue backsliding. Thus a lack of discernment is not only a mark of spiritual immaturity, but also a mark of those who are backsliding.

3) Lack of Discernment Is Proof of Spiritual Death

Those who have professed faith in Christ cannot backslide indefinitely. Sooner or later it will become clear that they are not believers at all and surely never were. The Bible does not tell us if the recipients of the letter to the Hebrews continued to fall away or if God graciously used this letter to draw them back to him. But Scripture tells us elsewhere what happens to those who harden their hearts against God, rejecting his good gifts. Romans 1:28–32 is a damning indictment of the unregenerate human heart. It shows with terrifying clarity the evil of which humans are capable. These verses make plain the extent of the sinfulness of those who have rejected the true God in favor of false gods of their own making:

> Since they did not see fit to acknowledge God, God gave them up to a debased mind to do what ought not to be done. They were filled with all manner of unrighteousness, evil, covetousness, malice. They are full of envy, murder, strife, deceit, maliciousness. They are gossips, slanderers, haters of God, insolent, haughty, boastful, inventors of evil, disobedient to parents, foolish, faithless, heartless, ruthless. Though they know God's decree that those who practice such things deserve to die, they not only do them but give approval to those who practice them.

These verses ought to strike terror in the heart of all who forsake God and ought to cause us all to pause and acknowledge the depth of the evil that inhabits the hearts of men. As men turn from God, he gives them up to do those things their hearts, filled with evil, cry out to do: envy, murder, hatred, gossip, boasting, and all manner of evil. And in the midst of this list is one word that seems almost unexpected.[4] God gives people up to *foolishness*. Most Bible translations render this word as "without understanding." One, the New King James Version, translates it as "undiscerning." Regardless of how it is rendered in English, this word points to a type of moral foolishness that should not be present in the life of one who considers himself a Christian. It points not only to the sinfulness of a lack of discernment, but to the inevitable conclusion that a lack of discernment, utter foolishness, is a mark of one who is spiritually dead and bankrupt.

A complete lack of discernment or lack of concern for the discipline of discernment is a mark of spiritual death. It is categorized with sins that somehow seem far more serious. That a lack of discernment appears in this list seems shocking, but it shows just how

---

[4] I am indebted to pastor Phillip Way for his series of articles called "Learn to Discern" (http://pastorway.blogspot.com/2006/06/failing-to-discern.html).

much God values discernment. An absolute lack of discernment and a lack of concern for discernment is sure proof of spiritual death.

We see also in 1 Corinthians 2:14 the dire consequences of ignoring discernment: "The natural person does not accept the things of the Spirit of God, for they are folly to him, and he is not able to understand them because they are spiritually discerned." Those who are unsaved, who do not have the Spirit of God within them, are unable to be discerning. The ways of God and the truths of God are utter foolishness to such people.

To lack discernment is to sin against God. It is an inevitable result of turning from him. It is easy to look at those who have turned from God and to look at their lustful and angry hearts and affirm that this is the result of their sin. When a Christian falls into moral sin he may well examine his life to determine how he has turned his back on God, but is the same true when he exhibits a lack of discernment? A wise pastor writes, "to willingly neglect the truth and to live with our eyes closed shut while good and evil stare us in the face is to sin against God, ourselves, our families, and our church. . . . Again, this is worth stating over and over again. It is the responsibility of every Christian to learn, to be discipled in the Word, so that we can know how to be discerning. To fail to discern is to walk in darkness."[5]

This is the bad news. Scripture portrays those who lack spiritual discernment in three ways: they are spiritually immature, they are backslidden, and they are dead. Those who lack discernment or do not care for it will fit into one of these three categories. These are the dangers of ignoring discernment.

But there is good news, too. The Bible declares that there are many benefits stored up for those who desire discernment, those who seek after it and practice it.

DISCERNMENT IS PROOF OF SPIRITUAL LIFE

We have seen that a lack of discernment is a mark of spiritual death. The Bible makes it clear that a person with no discernment is a per-

---

[5]Phillip Way, "Failing to Discern" (http://pastorway.blogspot.com/2006/06/failing-to-discern.html).

son who has not been saved. The opposite is equally true. A person who exhibits spiritual discernment shows that he has spiritual life. All those who are saved must begin to progress in their ability to discern. Proverbs 9:10 tells us, "The fear of the LORD is the beginning of wisdom, and the knowledge of the Holy One is insight." The word translated as "insight" is a Hebrew equivalent to "discernment." Solomon tells us here that to know God is to possess discernment and that knowledge of God is the very starting point for discernment. Those who fear the Lord, those who know God, must be discerning, for God himself is the very source of discernment. God is also our motive for discernment, for by living lives marked by discernment we bring honor and glory to his name.

The book of Ephesians also draws a clear line between spiritual discernment and spiritual life. Paul, having told his readers how they as Christians have left the kingdom of darkness, admonishes them now to "walk as children of light (for the fruit of light is found in all that is good and right and true), and try to discern what is pleasing to the Lord" (Eph. 5:8b–10). Those who know the Lord and have been brought into his kingdom of light will do their utmost to seek God's will in discerning what is pleasing to him. Where there is discernment, there is life.

DISCERNMENT IS PROOF OF SPIRITUAL GROWTH

Whereas a lack of discernment leads to backsliding, those who grow in discernment will necessarily grow spiritually. Jesus continually emphasized discernment during his ministry, sometimes scolding those who did not have it and sometimes commending those who did. Jesus scolded the disciples for not understanding, or discerning, the point of his miraculous feeding of the four thousand (see Mark 8:17–21). Although Jesus had just finished feeding a multitude, the disciples were concerned that they had no bread for themselves:

> And Jesus, aware of this, said to them, "Why are you discussing the fact that you have no bread? Do you not yet perceive or understand? Are your hearts hardened? Having eyes do you not see, and

having ears do you not hear? And do you not remember? When I
broke the five loaves for the five thousand, how many baskets full
of broken pieces did you take up?" They said to him, "Twelve."
"And the seven for the four thousand, how many baskets full of
broken pieces did you take up?" And they said to him, "Seven."
And he said to them, "Do you not yet understand?"

Jesus scolded the disciples for not understanding, or discerning,
what this miracle pointed to. Though they watched it unfold and ate
of the bread, they still did not understand just who Jesus was and
what he was going to accomplish. Their lack of growth kept them
from understanding. Their lack of discernment was a clear sign of
spiritual immaturity.

Conversely, in Matthew 13 the disciples asked Jesus why he
spoke so often in parables. Jesus explained his rationale and commended the disciples for their ability to understand the parables that
are so often hidden from others: "But blessed are your eyes, for they
see, and your ears, for they hear. Truly, I say to you, many prophets
and righteous people longed to see what you see, and did not see it,
and to hear what you hear, and did not hear it" (vv. 16–17). In this
case he commended his disciples for exhibiting a level of spiritual
maturity. Jesus declared the disciples blessed for their ability to see
and perceive. He declared them blessed for their ability to discern.
Their spiritual growth was marked by an increase in discernment.
Their ability to discern was an unequivocal testament to their spiritual growth.

DISCERNMENT IS PROOF OF SPIRITUAL MATURITY

Finally, just as a lack of discernment is a mark of spiritual immaturity, the presence of discernment is a sure mark of maturity. Again,
the author of Hebrews warns, "Solid food is for the mature, for
those who have their powers of discernment trained by constant
practice to distinguish good from evil" (Heb. 5:14). Christians
who are mature are those who have exercised discernment and
have learned how to distinguish good from evil. Spiritual maturity
is closely tied to discernment. You cannot have one without the

other. There are no Christians who are mature but undiscerning (see *figure 1*).

Figure 1
Discernment Equals Maturity

LACK OF DISCERNMENT	DISCERNMENT
Spiritual immaturity	Spiritual maturity
Backsliding	Spiritual growth
Spiritually dead	Spiritually alive

The Bible makes it clear: God expects and demands that we pursue and exhibit spiritual discernment. Healthy Christians—those who are alive, growing, and mature—are necessarily those who seek to honor God by discerning between what is good and what is evil.

THE DEPOSIT

One of my favorite television programs is *Antiques Roadshow*. The program affords people the opportunity to present their antique possessions—whether furniture, paintings, toys, or anything else—and to have them appraised by some of the world's foremost experts in antiquities. For every episode the producers single out ten or fifteen items and show an expert providing a detailed description and valuation of the item. Each section closes with the expert telling the owner just what the item is worth. It is always amusing to see eyes pop out or to see people jump up and down with excitement as they realize that they have in their possession an item worth tens or even hundreds of thousands of dollars. During every episode the viewer has opportunity to see "junk" transformed to treasure.

There is one segment from a particular episode that stands out in my mind, because it featured the most valuable item they had appraised to that point. An elderly gentleman from Tucson, Arizona, brought in an old blanket he had inherited several years before. He knew it was old and believed it had a little bit of value, perhaps a few hundred or even a couple of thousand dollars. After inheriting this blanket he had thrown it over the back of a rocking chair in his bedroom and had not often thought about it until presented with an opportunity to take it to the Roadshow.

With the blanket hanging on a rack behind them, the expert appraiser told the old man that his heart had stopped when he first saw it. As I watched the show, I could see the excitement written all over the expert's face and extending throughout his body. He could not stand still. He began to explain that the item was a Navajo chief's blanket that had been woven in the 1840s. In wonderful condition, it was one of the oldest, intact Navajo weaves to survive to the twenty-first century, and certainly one of only a tiny handful to exist outside of museum collections. He showed the fine detail of the weaving and even showed where it had been torn and repaired shortly after it was first made. I could see the excitement in his eyes as he looked at something he knew was extremely valuable. He knew that sitting before him was something more than a blanket—it was a rare national treasure of incredible value and historical significance.

The appraiser seemed to have trouble even beginning to convey to the audience the importance of this blanket. He left no doubt, though, when he told of its value. Because of its rarity and significance, he had no trouble assigning a value of somewhere between 350,000 and 500,000 dollars. This elderly gentleman had come to the show carrying a blanket worth almost a half-million dollars. He simply could not believe what he was hearing. Choked up and with tears pouring from his eyes he asked to hear the amount again. He looked as if he might pass out.

As the man walked out of the convention center where the show had been held, the blanket he had cavalierly carried in with him was now cradled carefully in his arms. He walked out of the building with security guards on either side of him, drove straight to a bank, and placed the blanket in a safe deposit box. What had been "junk," a mere accent to an old rocking chair, had been instantly transformed into a precious treasure.

When God saves his people, bringing us from death to life, he opens our eyes to love and appreciate the supreme treasure that is Jesus Christ. What had once been of little interest or significance is suddenly transformed into something of inestimable value and worth. The gospel message—the news of Jesus' miraculous birth, perfect life, substitutionary death, and glorious resurrection—is great and joyous news, and yet, for this very reason, it is under attack by the forces of evil. The eminent nineteenth-century pastor and author J. C. Ryle wrote of just some of the ways the gospel can be spoiled to us:

> You may spoil the Gospel by *substitution*. You have only to withdraw from the eyes of the sinner the grand object which the Bible proposes to faith,—Jesus Christ; and to substitute another object in His place . . . and the mischief is done. Substitute anything for Christ, and the Gospel is totally spoiled! . . .
>
> You may spoil the Gospel by *addition*. You have only to add to Christ, the grand object of faith, some other objects as equally worthy of honour, and the mischief is done. Add anything to Christ, and the Gospel ceases to be a pure Gospel! . . .
>
> You may spoil the Gospel by *interposition*. You have only to push something between Christ and the eye of the soul, to draw away the sinner's attention from the Saviour, and the mischief is done. . . .
>
> You may spoil the Gospel by *disproportion*. You have only to attach an exaggerated importance to the secondary things of Christianity, and a diminished importance to the first things, and the mischief is done. Once alter the proportion of the parts of truth, and truth soon becomes downright error! . . .
>
> You may completely spoil the Gospel by *confused and contradictory directions*. Complicated and obscure statements about faith, baptism, Church privileges, and the benefits of the Lord's Supper . . . are almost as bad as no statement at all![6]

The gospel can be spoiled, though not objectively, for it is an objective reality. Yet it can be spoiled by us and to us. We can modify the gospel, either deliberately or inadvertently, stripping it of its power and its glory. We can bring to people a counterfeit gospel that is no gospel at all. It is the discipline of discernment that God has provided us to guard the purity of the gospel.

---

[6]J. C. Ryle, "Evangelical Religion" (http://www.tracts.ukgo.com/ryle_evangelical_religion.htm).

Discernment, then, is not an end in itself. Rather, discernment is the means to a far greater and nobler end. By practicing spiritual discernment we guard the gospel, the message of eternal life. The apostle Paul, writing to his young protégé Timothy, called him to do just this in both of the letters to Timothy recorded in Scripture. "O Timothy, guard the deposit entrusted to you," Paul writes in 1 Timothy 6:20. In his next letter he reiterates, "By the Holy Spirit who dwells within us, guard the good deposit entrusted to you" (2 Tim. 1:14). Through the power of the Spirit, Timothy was to guard the gospel.

This word *deposit* is taken from the ancient world. In the age before personal safes and safe deposit boxes, a person who was going to be away for some time might ask another to care for a treasured possession. He would entrust this possession to another, depositing it to him, and this person was bound by a sacred oath to protect it.[7] In his letters to Timothy, Paul, who knows that he will not always be able to encourage and mentor Timothy, entrusts to him the gospel message. Timothy would be expected to guard this message and to find worthy, godly Christians to whom he could in turn entrust it. And so the gospel has been protected and has carried from one generation to the next through the long, storied history of the church. And so it has been handed in trust to you and to me and to all who believe.

John Stott, in his introduction to his commentary on 2 Timothy, says this:

> The church of our day urgently needs to heed the message of this second letter of Paul to Timothy. For all around us we see Christians and churches relaxing their grasp of the gospel, fumbling it, in danger of letting it drop from their hands altogether. A new generation of young Timothys is needed, who will guard the sacred deposit of the gospel, who are determined to proclaim it and are prepared to suffer for it, and who will pass it on pure and uncorrupted to the generation which in due course will rise up to follow them.[8]

---

[7]William B. Barcley, *1 & 2 Timothy* (Faverdale North, UK: Evangelical Press, 2005), 210–11.
[8]John Stott, *The Message of 2 Timothy* (Leicester: Inter-Varsity Press, 1973), 22.

God has given us the gospel in trust. He has deposited it to our account and expects that we will guard this priceless, precious treasure. God has entrusted to us something of infinite worth and unsurpassed beauty. He has not left us to our own devices, but he has provided for us the Holy Spirit, that with his help we may be faithful in guarding the gospel of Jesus Christ. Spiritual discernment allows us to keep the gospel central and allows us to see and guard against error. Spiritual discernment is absolutely crucial to the one who would understand and heed the gospel. Nothing less than the gospel is at stake.

THE CALL

As we saw at the beginning of this chapter, King Solomon knew the importance of discernment. The early verses of Proverbs are a call for both wisdom and discernment:

> My son, if you receive my words
>   and treasure up my commandments with you,
> making your ear attentive to wisdom
>   and inclining your heart to understanding;
> yes, if you call out for insight
>   and raise your voice for understanding,
> if you seek it like silver
>   and search for it as for hidden treasures,
> then you will understand the fear of the LORD
>   and find the knowledge of God. (Prov. 2:1–5)

We are to incline our hearts to discernment and to cry out for it. We should desire spiritual maturity, spiritual growth, and spiritual life. We can only have these wonderful benefits if we have discernment. We serve a God who stands ready and willing to bestow this gift upon those who seek after it.

Proverbs 2 is a father's call to his son to embrace and treasure discernment. There are few things that are as important, as precious, as spiritual discernment. The Bible cries for you to seek after it so you can live, so you can grow, and so you can mature in your faith. Will you answer the call?

KEY THOUGHT

The Bible teaches there is a clear relationship between spiritual discernment and spiritual maturity. For a Christian to be mature, he must also be discerning. Those who are not discerning must be immature, backsliding, or dead. Conversely, those who exhibit discernment must be alive, growing, and mature. It is clear from Scripture that all Christians are expected to pursue discernment, for the Bible cries out repeatedly for us to do so. It is the responsibility of each Christian to heed and to answer the call and so to guard the deposit God has entrusted to us.

the CHALLENGE of DISCERNMENT

"Blessed are you when others revile you and persecute you and utter all kinds of evil against you falsely on my account. Rejoice and be glad, for your reward is great in heaven, for so they persecuted the prophets who were before you."
MATTHEW 5:11–12

DAVID VETTER IS KNOWN AS "the bubble boy." Born in Shenandoah, Texas, in 1971, David suffered from a rare genetic disorder known as severe combined immune deficiency syndrome (or SCIDS). This is a disease in which the body's immune system is crippled from birth, leaving the patient at extreme risk of sickness and disease. Knowing that he would be born with this condition, within twenty seconds of his birth doctors placed Vetter within a protective bubble designed to serve as a safe and germ-free environment for him. Anything that was to be passed into the bubble first had to be painstakingly disinfected with special cleaning agents. The occasional doctor or nurse who entered had to be completely free of germs and bacteria. David lived in this bubble for nearly the whole of his thirteen years before dying of complications from a bone marrow transplant. All that time, he lived in a bubble where the air he breathed was carefully filtered, and everything he touched was disinfected. His body, unable to protect itself, was guarded because it was not allowed to come into contact with anything foreign or dangerous. He did not need an immune system as long as he stayed within this bubble.

Many Christians wish they could live in a bubble similar to this—a bubble that would protect them from false teaching and allow them to avoid having to develop or use spiritual discernment. Every teaching they encounter would be sterilized, guaranteed to be free of any falsehood. Any person entering the bubble would be perfectly disinfected from false doctrine, bringing in only the truth. Yet this is not the world we live in. We live in a world that is in direct opposition to Christianity. Just as germs are constantly waging war on our bodies, false doctrine is constantly raging against our faith. God has provided us with discernment to enable us to withstand these attacks.

It was tempting, as I wrote this book, to include a chapter arguing that Christians today are having a crisis in discernment. It was tempting to look at Christian books, programs, and leaders and to point to the multitudes of examples proving just how far Christians have drifted from the Bible's standards. I concluded, though, that such a chapter was unnecessary. Proving that the church is suffering from a lack of discernment would be like proving that the sky is blue—it would be to prove something that is, unfortunately, obvious to anyone who cares to seek evidence of it. But while it might be a waste to prove the church's lack of discernment, it seems valuable to look further and seek to understand why discernment is a particularly difficult skill to exercise in our day and our culture.

Of course it has never been easy to be discerning. Discernment is a skill that must be sharpened with long years of practice. Hebrews 5:14, a verse we have already seen, tells us that discernment comes to those who "by constant practice [work] to distinguish good from evil." While it is a discipline that requires practice, discernment is a skill that does not tend to make us popular, for, as we will soon see, it requires us to make clear and unwavering distinctions between what is good and what is evil. The words of Jesus in Matthew 10:34–37 warn about the consequences of those who follow him:

"Do not think that I have come to bring peace to the earth. I have not come to bring peace, but a sword. For I have come to set a man against his father, and a daughter against her mother, and a daughter-in-law against her mother-in-law. And a person's enemies will be those of his own household. Whoever loves father or mother more than me is not worthy of me, and whoever loves son or daughter more than me is not worthy of me."

With discernment comes division. A person who seeks to be discerning must be willing to suffer the effects of this division. It will divide not only believer from unbeliever, but it may even divide a discerning believer from one who is undiscerning. It will separate the mature from the immature, the naïve from the prudent.

There are several forces that work against us as we attempt to be men and women of discernment. There are internal forces stemming from our sinful human natures; there are spiritual forces that seek to promote deception; and there are external forces originating in the culture around us. In this chapter we will examine each of these challenges and attempt to understand why Christians today do not place a greater emphasis on the practice of discernment.

INTERNAL INFLUENCES

"The heart is deceitful above all things, and desperately sick; who can understand it?" asks the prophet Jeremiah (Jer. 17:9). From the moment Adam and Eve defied God and ate of the fruit that he commanded them to avoid, the hearts of all humans have been plagued with sin. It is almost impossible to overestimate the human propensity for evil. Like moths to a flame humans are drawn to sin. Our sinful hearts delight in all that is evil and ungodly. When we become Christians, we are given new hearts, hearts that seek after God. Yet the evil continues to dwell within. We engage in a lifelong struggle to identify where evil lurks in our hearts and to tear it out by the roots. Even while we seek after godliness, there is a part of us that yearns to return to our former master and to cast off all traces of God's presence in our lives. Were it not for God's grace, none of us would make any progress in this Christian life.

J. R. R. Tolkien seems to have understood this struggle, and his series *The Lord of the Rings* provides a powerful metaphor of it. In these books Tolkien describes a ring of power, a single ring into which the evil sorcerer Sauron has poured all of his wrath, fury, and evil. This ring has almost a mind of its own and desires to return to its master. As Sauron's minions search for this ring, Frodo, who has inherited it and now seeks to destroy it, finds himself drawn to these evil Ringwraiths. The ring, which he wears on a chain around his neck, pulls him toward the power of evil. This ring desires to return to its wicked master. At the same time, it pollutes the kind, good, and naïve Frodo with its evil. When given the opportunity to throw this ring into the depths of Mount Doom, destroying it forever, Frodo finds himself unable to part with it, despite the pain and torment it has caused him. He hates this evil ring and hates what it has done to him. And yet he cannot let it go. He wants to keep it, to tame it. In the end it can only be destroyed when it is torn from his grasp. And this is so often how Christians relate to sin. Even though we have been saved and regenerated by the Holy Spirit, we hold on to our sin, for something in us is still drawn to it.

As we seek after discernment, a good and godly desire, our sinful natures will fight against us. We will soon discover a part of ourselves that does not want to make clear distinctions between what is good and evil, and a part of ourselves that does not want to be committed to what is good and right and true. And so the first enemy we must overcome in our discipline of discernment is ourselves.

Thankfully, we are not alone in this battle. When we were brought from death to life, when we became Christians, we were given the Holy Spirit, who now dwells within us. The Spirit's task is to renew our hearts continually and to empower us to fight for the goal of being conformed to the image of Jesus Christ. If we are to be a people of discernment, we need to begin our pursuit by crying out to the Spirit and asking him to help and to guide us as we seek after discernment.

SPIRITUAL INFLUENCES

While we must be prepared to fight against the internal influences of our fallen natures, we must also deal with external, spiritual influences. Satan, once the mightiest of the angels, is now the devil on the prowl for those who have forsaken him and who are seeking after God. Satan seeks to lead us astray. His tactics rarely change, for since the dawn of human history they have proven remarkably effective. Satan seeks to lead us astray, to deceive us, by offering us a counterfeit version of the truth. Satan offers something that resembles the truth but is actually error. He is crafty and subtle, offering something that seems so close yet is still so far away. "Did God *really* say?" were his words to Eve, and they are the words he continues to use today.

I recently read C. S. Lewis's *The Lion, the Witch and the Wardrobe* to my two older children. Though my parents had read this story to me when I was a child, I had not read it in many years and had forgotten many of the details. As I read it aloud, I was struck time and again by the insightful ways in which Lewis describes sin and evil. Significantly, the White Witch, the story's primary evil character, is unable to create and so relies instead on imitation. Part of her magic is "that she could make things look like what they aren't."[1] The winter imposed upon the land of Narnia is not a real winter but a mere imitation or perversion of a real one; the Turkish Delight she gives to Edmund is her imitation of ordinary food; the sledge she rides in is understood by many to be a deliberate imitation of the one used by Father Christmas. It is "a counterfeit, exactly like the real thing but a cheat. . . . Evil can only parody goodness, it cannot invent new forms of real beauty and joy. That is why in fairy tales you have to beware of attractive disguises—nice old crones selling apples in the forest, say, or angels of light."[2] This is a recurring theme in the story —the forces of evil attempting to deceive the innocent by counterfeiting what is good and right and true. By looking at the world of Narnia, we

---

[1]C. S. Lewis, *The Lion, the Witch and the Wardrobe* (New York: HarperCollins, 1950), 143.
[2]Thomas Howard, as quoted in Devin Brown, *Inside Narnia* (Grand Rapids, MI: Baker Books, 2005), 65.

see that C. S. Lewis had profound insights into the way evil functions in our world.

Consider an example of Satan's subtle works of counterfeiting and undermining the truth. The book of John begins in this way: "In the beginning was the Word, and the Word was with God, and the Word was God" (John 1:1). We learn a great deal from these few words. We see that Jesus is eternal, for he (the Word) existed in the beginning, so that before God created anything, Jesus already was. We learn about Jesus' divinity, for he was with God and really was God. These verses are critical to the Christian understanding of the Trinity and the person of Jesus.

But let's now look at the translation of these verses used by Jehovah's Witnesses in their New World Translation. "In the beginning was the Word, and the Word was with God, and the Word was a god." Once again, we can learn a great deal from these few words. We see that Jesus existed in the beginning, that Jesus was with God, and that Jesus was *a* god. And right here, though it is a single word, a single letter, a single indefinite article, the word *a* makes all the difference. Where John 1:1 clearly affirms the divinity of Jesus Christ, the Bible of the Jehovah's Witnesses denies this critical doctrine, teaching instead that Jesus was merely one of many gods created by the Father. Where an accurate rendition of this verse teaches that Jesus is eternal, the counterfeit translation makes him a created being. The difference is subtle but profound. It is the difference between beautiful truth and gross error. It is the difference between salvation and damnation. And this is how Satan works, always subtle, always crafty, always seeking to draw us away from what is true.

Satan is fully committed to our downfall and is committed to keeping us confused. He seeks to cause chaos and destruction by leading us away from discernment. He and his hordes of fallen angels seek to blur distinctions, to introduce subtle error, and to introduce what is ungodly to the church. In our fight for discernment we must battle against the spiritual forces arrayed against us. Thankfully Scripture is not silent and describes for us the "whole armor of God":

> Take up the whole armor of God, that you may be able to with-
> stand in the evil day, and having done all, to stand firm. Stand
> therefore, having fastened on the belt of truth, and having put
> on the breastplate of righteousness, and, as shoes for your feet,
> having put on the readiness given by the gospel of peace. In all cir-
> cumstances take up the shield of faith, with which you can extin-
> guish all the flaming darts of the evil one; and take the helmet of
> salvation, and the sword of the Spirit, which is the word of God,
> praying at all times in the Spirit, with all prayer and supplication.
> (Eph. 6:13–18a)

We have truth, righteousness, faith, salvation, and the Spirit to
guard us. We have the Word of God to battle for us. Through it all
we pray to the Spirit to protect and guide us against the schemes of
the devil. In this way we can fight against and overcome the spiritual
forces that are set against us and committed to our downfall. We can
wage war against and defeat the spiritual forces that seek to lead us
away from discernment by offering a clever and subtle counterfeit
of the truth.

CULTURAL INFLUENCES

Just as Christians must be prepared to deal with influences that
come from within and from the spirit realm, we must also be prepared to deal with influences arising from the culture in which we
live. We inhabit a fallen world, one that, though under the power
and authority of God, is opposed to him. It should come as no
surprise that even though we are called to live within this culture,
the culture itself hates God and seeks to destroy those who love
him. And yet this culture has influenced the church, perhaps more
than the church has influenced the culture. There are at least four
cultural influences that have led to a decline in discernment among
Christians.

Secular Worldview

Worldview is a word derived from the German *weltanschauung* that
means "look onto the world." It describes, quite simply, a way of

looking at the world. Every person has a worldview, which acts "like a mental map that tells us how to navigate the world effectively."[3] A worldview can be derived from any kind of ideology or influence. It can be Marxist, Darwinian, postmodern, or biblical. The one absolute truth regarding worldview is that every person has one. In the Introduction to her book *Total Truth*, Nancy Pearcey discusses the burgeoning Christian interest in the topic of worldview:

> Just a few years ago, when I began work on that earlier volume [*How Now Shall We Live?*], using the term *worldview* was not on anyone's list of good conversation openers. To tell people that you were writing a book on *worldview* was to risk glazed stares and a quick change in subject. But today as I travel around the country, I sense an eagerness among evangelicals to move beyond a purely privatized faith, applying biblical principles to areas like work, business, and politics. Flip open any number of Christian publications and you're likely to find half a dozen advertisements for *worldview* conferences, *worldview* institutes, and *worldview* programs. Clearly the term itself has strong marketing cachet these days, which signals a deep hunger among Christians for an overarching framework to bring unity to their lives.[4]

Pearcey addressed that hunger in her book and taught many people all they know on the topic. Underlying the book was the sad fact that the worldview of many who profess to be Christians is no different from that of those who do not. Research by George Barna has determined that as few as 9 percent of those who consider themselves born-again Christians have a Christian worldview premised upon these six basic truths of the Bible: (1) Jesus Christ lived a sinless life; (2) God is the all-powerful and all-knowing Creator of the universe and he stills rules it today; (3) salvation is a gift from God and cannot be earned; (4) Satan is real; (5) Christians have a responsibility to share their faith in Christ with other people; and (6) the Bible is accurate in all of its teachings.[5]

---

[3]Nancy Pearcey, *Total Truth: Liberating Christianity from Its Cultural Captivity* (Wheaton, IL: Crossway Books, 2005), 23.
[4]Ibid., 17.
[5]George Barna, "A Biblical Worldview Has a Radical Effect on a Person's Life"(http://www.barna.org/ FlexPage.aspx?Page=BarnaUpdate&BarnaUpdateID=154).

Sadly, many who consider themselves Christian have a world-view that is completely inconsistent with their profession of faith. It is a worldview premised not on the truths revealed in the Bible but on a person's flawed understanding of the world. It is ultimately a worldview rooted in a person's own sinfulness. The worldview we see around us is one that refuses to delineate an antithesis between good and evil. Conversely, a biblical worldview is rooted in an affirmation of the opposing forces of good and evil.

Biblical language is filled with examples of this antithesis: clean versus unclean, saved versus unsaved, good versus wicked, chosen versus "not chosen." The words the Bible uses in the original languages to describe discernment, as we will see in a later chapter, are rooted in this distinction. Discernment itself is rooted in the understanding that there is good and bad, that there are God's ways and other ways. A secular worldview, on the other hand, teaches that truth exists along a continuum. Truth is subjective; it is relative. One author says about the secular worldview:

> Every idea is a shade of gray. There is no right and wrong or true and false, but only shades of right and wrong or true and false spread along a continuum. The poles of this continuum are extended so far out towards the wings that for all practical purposes they are unattainable and therefore worthless. Nothing, then, is wholly right or wrong. All is relative; most of it is subjective.[6]

People simply do not "think Christianly." Os Guiness says, "Thinking Christianly is not simply thinking by Christians" and is not thinking by Christians "about Christian topics" or "adopting a 'Christian line' on every issue." Rather, thinking Christianly is "thinking by Christians about anything and everything in a consistent Christian way."[7]

This secular worldview is prevalent within the church. This unbiblical worldview encourages a secular mindset that in turn rejects discernment as unnecessarily divisive and discerning Christians as those who cause schisms within the body of Christ.

---

[6]Jay E. Adams, *A Call to Discernment* (Eugene, OR: Harvest House, 1987), 30.
[7]Os Guiness, *Fit Bodies, Fat Minds* (Grand Rapids, MI: Baker Books, 1994), 135–36.

True discernment can be founded only upon a Christian, biblical worldview that allows us to affirm the importance of the antithesis between good and evil. This worldview will allow us to think Christianly and to see the ugliness of error and the beauty of total truth.

A Low View of Scripture

Just as many Christians have abandoned a Christian worldview, many have abandoned the doctrines of Scripture. Many Christians have too low a view of the power and uniqueness of the Bible. They have absorbed the culture's skepticism and disregard for any person or book that claims authority over them.

In the last book he completed before his death in 2000, James Montgomery Boice, considered by many to be among the greatest preachers of the twentieth century, wrote about the five *solas* of the Reformation—the doctrines through which Protestantism was defined. The first of these, *sola scriptura*, or Scripture alone, is foundational to all of Christian theology. The Cambridge Declaration, formulated by the Alliance of Confessing Evangelicals, defines the doctrine in this way: "We reaffirm the inerrant Scripture to be the sole source of written divine revelation, which alone can bind the conscience. The Bible alone teaches all that is necessary for our salvation from sin and is the standard by which all Christian behavior must be measured." *Sola scriptura* declares that the Bible is the one and only perfect measure God has given to us as our guide in matters of life and faith.

Thirty years ago, the doctrine of the Bible's inerrancy, the doctrine which states that the Bible is without error, came under attack from both within the church and without. Protestant leaders such as Boice, J. I. Packer, R.C. Sproul, and Francis Schaeffer began an organization to clarify the Bible's teaching about itself and to defend it against those who sought to defraud it of its unique position. This battle was fought and largely won. Yet in his last book, written many years later, Boice had this to say: "Inerrancy is not the most critical issue facing the church today. The most serious issue, I believe, is the Bible's *sufficiency*."[8]

---

[8]James Montgomery Boice, *Whatever Happened to the Gospel of Grace?* (Wheaton, IL: Crossway Books, 2001), 72.

Dr. Boice's words are true. While all Christians are eager to embrace the Bible and to treat it as a precious possession, few are willing to give to it the preeminence it demands for itself. Charges of bibliolatry, or Bible worship, are thrown about with reckless abandon. People read and obey the Bible on their terms, expecting it to govern only what they allow it to. And yet the Bible demands that we allow it to be sufficient to address all areas of life and practice, whether evangelism, sanctification, guidance, social reform, or discernment.

Almost every evangelical church would somehow include in its statement of faith that they believe in *sola scriptura*, the doctrine stating that the Bible is our only perfect standard of right and wrong. Most of these churches do believe in such crucial doctrines as the Bible's authority, inspiration, and inerrancy. However, few would believe and put into practice the doctrine of the Bible's sufficiency. The evidence of this is visible in churches all around us. Many churches no longer look to the Bible as being the key to evangelism. Instead they put their trust in music, drama, outreach programs, and less imposing but more attractive church buildings. When people do come to church, they are not challenged by the gospel. Many churches no longer look to the Bible as their guide to counseling, opting instead to follow the latest methods of psychology. In so doing they deny that the Bible is truly sufficient to guide us in even these matters. And the examples could go on and on.

When we have rejected the doctrine of the sufficiency of Scripture, we allow Christians to depend on things other than the Bible as their guide to matters of life and faith. In particular, people begin to depend upon mysticism, upon ways of supposedly knowing God apart from the Bible. They look inward for *intrinsic* wisdom rather than outward to the Bible for its *extrinsic* wisdom. They forsake biblical reason in favor of feelings, voices, visions, or other subjective means of supposedly knowing God. This is a deadly error, for spiritual discernment must be founded upon God's objective revelation of himself in Scripture. We can only judge between what is wrong and what is right when we know what God says to be true. We can know this only from Scripture.

A Low View of Theology

The word *theology* has been much maligned in recent years. Both Christians and unbelievers have often rejected it, believing that theology is a somewhat less-than-noble pursuit. Theology is increasingly portrayed as the realm of fundamentalists—dangerous adherents to Christianity whose fanaticism makes others suspicious and distrustful. Practice is deemed important, underlying beliefs optional.

In the introduction to his book *No Place for Truth*, David F. Wells writes about a college-level class he teaches in introductory theology. One year he spent the opening day of this class waxing eloquent about the necessity of studying this discipline. Though he spoke with many students after that class, one conversation with a young man has stayed in his mind and even provided the impetus to write the book: "He told me that he was one of those I had described who felt petrified by the prospect of having to take this course. As a matter of fact, he said, he had had a mighty struggle with his conscience about it. Was it right to spend so much money on a course of study that was so irrelevant to his desire to minister to people in the Church?"[9] And Richard Phillips writes, "Theology bores today's Christians, which is another way of saying we are bored with God himself."[10]

Theology has become a bad word in many Christian circles just as it was a bad word in the mind of the young man Wells encountered. Theology is often linked in people's minds with cold, dead religion that cares more about principles and matters of the head than deeds and matters of the heart. It is associated with fundamentalism and with cold conservatism. Yet if we look at the meaning and etymology of the word, we cannot help but conclude that God requires all Christians to be theologians.

The word *theology* is derived from two Greek words. The root *theos* means "God" and the suffix *-ology* comes from the Greek word for "speak." So what theology really means is "speaking of God" or, what has become the more accurate definition, "the study of God." That doesn't sound so bad, does it? Surely no Christian

---

[9]David F. Wells, *No Place for Truth, or, Whatever Happened to Evangelical Theology?* (Grand Rapids, MI: Eerdmans, 1993), 4.
[10]Richard Phillips, *Hebrews* (Phillipsburg, NJ: P&R, 2006), 179.

can deny that we are called by God to learn more about him and to study his ways. The process of sanctification is just that—learning more and more about God and his requirements for our lives. We must then mold our lives to fit into that image. We must know theology so we can allow it to govern our actions.

Sadly, though, many Christians have separated theology from practice, knowledge of God from their practice of serving him. Some Christians delight in their ignorance, claiming that they don't want theology; they just want to love Jesus. These people tend to build their faith upon feelings and experiences rather than upon the truths of the Bible.

As theology has declined, so has *systematic* theology—the study of themes in Scripture. This discipline used to lie at the heart of much seminary training and much preparation for the ministry. Sadly, today this is often no longer the case. But Christianity is not a faith that can be taken à la carte. It is not a faith that allows its adherents to pick and choose which elements they would like to accept and which they would prefer to reject. Christianity is nothing if not systematic. For us to understand what the Bible teaches, we must examine it systematically, seeking to learn how one doctrine builds upon another. We cannot have right theology if we are not systematic, and we cannot be systematic if we do not look to Scripture to guide our theology. We must have both.

When theology in general, and systematic theology in particular, are downplayed, it is no longer possible to defend beliefs that are structured according to systematic, logical, biblical principles. We are left instead with a hodgepodge of disparate, sometimes contradictory beliefs that bear little resemblance to biblical Christianity. As theology falls out of favor in the culture, so too does it fall out of favor in the church. This makes the pursuit of discernment ever more difficult and ever more unpopular.

A Low View of God

Many Christians—whether through their own ignorance or as a result of being poorly trained—downplay the holiness of God.

God's name is maligned and blasphemed in the culture around us, and it seems that Christians have increasingly absorbed the world's understanding of a God who is fun, who exists for our benefit, and who can be the butt of endless jokes.

When believers do not understand God's holiness and allow this doctrine to shape their faith, they cannot understand his hatred of all that is sinful and, thus, the need for discernment. God's holiness lies at the very heart of the need for discernment. Our passion for God's holiness, our desire to keep ourselves pure from sin, will motivate our practice of discernment. The greater our understanding of God's holiness, the greater will be our understanding of the importance of discerning truth from error. We will desire to cast off all that is wrong so that we can be unsullied, unspoiled by sin.

Throughout Scripture God reveals himself as holy. God's holiness is his quality of being separate from or apart from all that is evil. He is, thus, perfect—free from any kind of moral evil or imperfection. Morally and ethically, God is without any trace of sin. Because he is holy and is the very source of all holiness and perfection, God cannot tolerate any manner of evil. Hebrews 12:14 teaches that no one who is unholy will be able to see the Lord or to stand in his presence. It is for this very reason that Jesus Christ was made to be a sacrifice for us. Only through the life, death, and resurrection of the Son of God could sinners like you and me be made holy and worthy of God's presence. In his death Christ's holiness was given to those who believe in him so that they were given the ability to stand before him and to see him someday face-to-face. As we saw earlier in this chapter, the life of the Christian is now marked by a continual striving after this holiness as we cast off all that is evil and seek to replace it with that which is good. We seek to honor God by removing from our lives the very sins that necessitated the death of his dear Son. We do this because God is holy and because we, too, want to be holy.

As we have lost sight of the holiness of God, we have lost our emphasis on *personal* holiness. The Bible calls upon us to seek to imitate God in all his perfections. The missionary David Livingstone

used to pray that he "might imitate Christ in all His inimitable perfections." This should be the prayer of all Christians, that we might
more and more be conformed to the image of Jesus Christ.

The low view of God that pervades our culture has influenced
the church. We have too low a view of God, and especially of his
holiness. When God's holy nature is downplayed or ignored, so too
is the importance of discernment. We must continually pray that
God will give us grace to imitate him in his holiness. We can only do
this when we are willing and able to discern between good and bad,
truth and error. Only when we recover the Bible's teaching on God's
holiness will we be able to guard against the cultural influences that
seek to undermine his very character.

Spiritual discernment has never been an easy calling. Throughout
the Bible we see men and women of discernment being persecuted,
mocked, and reviled both by those within the church and those
outside of it. Just as the judges, prophets, and apostles suffered for
their discerning faith, so those who seek to emphasize discernment
in our time can expect to suffer. They can expect to face opposition
and disagreement from those who claim Christ and those who do
not. They will face opposition from their own sinful hearts and from
spiritual forces. And still, like the apostle Paul, they must persevere,
straining forward to what lies ahead and pressing on toward the
goal for the prize of the upward call of God in Christ Jesus (Phil.
3:13–14). They must believe that to serve and honor God—to think
Christianly, to treasure the Bible, to seek to know God as he is, and
to humble themselves before his holiness—is a prize far greater than
anything they may suffer.

KEY THOUGHT

Because discernment is a good and noble pursuit, it is one that has
been opposed on all fronts. It will continue to be opposed by our
sinful natures, by satanic forces, and by cultural influences. As
Christians we must stand firm against all of these forces, trusting in
God to equip and to sustain us, for while discernment is a difficult
calling, it is one with ultimate benefits.

chapter three

DEFINING DISCERNMENT

Abhor what is evil; hold fast to what is good.
ROMANS 12:9B

THE ISSUE OF HOMOSEXUAL MARRIAGE has electrified the church. I live in Canada, a nation that has already passed laws allowing homosexuals to marry and to have the same spousal rights as heterosexual couples. Of all the arguments against homosexual marriage, it seems to me that the most convincing is simply this: the biblical definition of marriage does not allow it. As the one who created the institution of marriage, only God has the right to define it. He has done this clearly in Scripture and has told us that marriage is the union of one man and one woman. We cannot and must not extend this definition or redefine it. This is not ours to do. In the controversy surrounding homosexual marriage, the definition of marriage proves that there can be no such thing as gay marriage.

Definitions matter. There is a great deal of disagreement about how best to define *discernment*. A quick search through books and web sites dealing with discernment reveals a wide variety of definitions, some secular, some Christian, and others New Age. One of the definitions says discernment is "perception of that which is obscure," and another says it's "the ability to feel or perceive something with the mind and the senses." Several definitions of discernment revolve around decision making, calling it "prayerful reflection and discussion before making a major decision" or "discovering, with God's help, God's will for our lives." A more thorough definition reads, "Discernment is a process of prayerful reflection which leads a person or community to understanding of God's call at a given time or in particular circumstances of life. It involves listening to God in all the ways God communicates with us: in prayer, in the scriptures, through the Church and the world, in personal experience, and in other people."[1] I would suggest that this final definition most accurately represents what many Christians think of when they consider discernment. To many followers of Christ discernment is a gift or ability that equips us to make good and wise decisions. In this view those who make good decisions in life are discerning. Conversely, people who make poor decisions in life are those who lack discernment.

While the Bible makes it clear that discernment relates to decision making, my studies of this topic have led me to see that a definition that goes little further than this is simply too narrow, for biblical discernment looks beyond the *will* of God to the *truth* of God. We can only know God's will when we first know God's truth, for what God desires and requires of us must always be consistent with his character. Wise decisions are those that are made on the firm basis of what is true about God and, thus, what is true about the world, about life, and about ourselves. Those who make decisions that honor God are those who have invested effort in studying what God says to be true. Hebrew scholar Bruce Waltke bemoans the fact that so few people understand that to know God's will we must first know God's truth. "The tragedy is that most of the young people in the church at large do not know it. They're trying to find God's will, often very sincerely, but don't know what the Bible says."[2]

Because God *is* truth, knowing God and knowing truth are inseparable. If we wish to know truth, we must know God. If we

---

[1] Vocations.ca, "Common Terms" (http://www.vocations.ca/What is a vocation/common terms.php).
[2] Source unlocated.

know God, we will also know truth. We see this with great clarity
in the book of Proverbs. Solomon, whom we have already seen as
the most wise and discerning man who ever lived, wrote "The fear
of the LORD is the beginning of knowledge; fools despise wisdom
and instruction" (Prov. 1:7). Knowledge, not as an end in itself, but
as an end to better know, understand, and serve God, begins with
the character of God. When we think of Proverbs we typically think
of the section of the book known as "the proverbs of Solomon"—
those pithy statements found in the latter portions of the book that
give us much cause to laugh, much cause to pause, much cause to
ponder. But before we get to these pithy sayings, we find that the
book first lays and then builds upon the firm foundation of personal
character. The initial chapters of Proverbs, the first nine, are given to
us for this very reason, that we may develop character. Before God
will address conduct, he chooses to address character. Once he has
molded and shaped our hearts, he is ready to train us in wisdom
and understanding. Truth comes first and application of the truth
follows later. And so we must know God's truth before we can know
God's will.

WISDOM

Before we define discernment, it will prove helpful to briefly discuss
wisdom. We saw from the life of Solomon in 1 Kings 3:9 that wisdom was a prerequisite to discernment, for though he asked God for
discernment he was given *both* wisdom and discernment. The latter
seems to depend on the former.

The central thesis of the book of Proverbs, and indeed, of all of
the Bible's wisdom literature is this: "The fear of the LORD is the
beginning of knowledge; fools despise wisdom and instruction"
(Proverbs 1:7). Wisdom is the application of the fear of God to life;
it is living in such a way that we esteem God above all else. A man
who is wise is first a man who fears God. This is not a terrified,
horrified fear, as in the fear of a child for a monster or an abusive
father, but a fear based on a realistic understanding of the infinite
gap between God and man in holiness and knowledge. Wisdom is

not knowledge for its own sake, like the knowledge of the ancient Greeks, but knowledge that leads to a greater understanding of the meaning of life and how life is to be lived. In *The Wisdom of Proverbs, Job & Ecclesiastes*, Derek Kidner writes of the Bible's wisdom literature, "Where the bulk of the Old Testament calls us simply to obey and to believe, this part of it . . . summons us to think hard as well as humbly; to keep our eyes open, to use our conscience and our common sense, and not to shirk the most disturbing questions."[3] Wisdom is attained and enhanced as we think deeply and humbly about how we are to serve God.

According to Bruce Waltke wisdom refers to "masterful understanding," "skill," or "expertise."[4] The word relates to the mind or to the intellect but is more than mere knowledge. Wisdom is more than merely attaining or collecting facts. A person may have a great deal of knowledge and may be a master of trivia but still not have wisdom, for there is a moral and ethical dimension to wisdom. Wisdom is not an end in itself, but a means to molding human behavior in a way that pleases God. "It is a way of thinking about reality that enables one to pursue what is good in life. Through wisdom, God reveals what the values of life are and how they may be achieved."[5] Said more plainly, "wisdom is the skill of living a godly life."[6] Wisdom allows us to pursue what is good in life, not as judged by our standards but as judged by the Creator. Wisdom allows us to see what is important to God, what values he gives us for our own benefit, and it allows him to teach us how we can pursue them. Wisdom allows us to rightly use knowledge; it allows us to be discerning. Said otherwise, wisdom is knowledge rightly understood.

For the purposes of this book, I frequently draw a line between wisdom and discernment, though in the Bible this distinction is not always perfectly clear. At times the Bible seems to speak of wisdom and discernment as two separate entities, two separate skills. At

---

[3]Derek Kidner, *The Wisdom of Proverbs, Job and Ecclesiastes* (Leicester: Inter-Varsity Press, 1985), 11.
[4]Bruce Waltke, *The Book of Proverbs* (Grand Rapids, MI: Eerdmans, 2004), 76.
[5]R. C. Sproul, in *Reformation Study Bible* (Lake Mary, FL: Ligonier Ministries), 872.
[6]John MacArthur, in *MacArthur Study Bible* (Nashville: Thomas Nelson, 2006), 865.

other times it seems loath to differentiate between them. I would suggest this simply points to the fact that wisdom and discernment are inexorably connected as with the two sides of a single coin. One depends on the other; the former cannot be had without the latter. Still, by studying Proverbs and other portions of the Bible it often seems that discernment is a subset of wisdom. There seems to be a progression from knowledge, which refers to bare facts, to wisdom, which refers to understanding moral and ethical dimensions of facts and data, to discernment, which is the application of wisdom. Wisdom is a prerequisite to discernment. Discernment is wisdom in action.

We can see an example of the difference between wisdom and discernment in Proverbs 26:4–5, which reads, "Answer not a fool according to his folly, lest you be like him yourself. Answer a fool according to his folly, lest he be wise in his own eyes." Solomon provided two Proverbs that seem to stand in direct contradiction to each other. One cautions against answering the accusations or supposed wisdom of a fool while the other suggests that this is exactly what the fool needs in order to teach him humility. It is wisdom to know these things. A wise man will know that there are times when a person needs to be answered and there are times when it is better to remain silent. A discerning man, though, will know *when* he should give an answer and when he should know better. The wise man knows that both of these situations can be true, but it is the discerning man who understands which is best to use in a given situation. Discernment skillfully applies wisdom to a real-life situation.

As with wisdom, the biblical concept of discernment must be distinguished from the mere attainment of knowledge or the gathering of data. In the biblical paradigm, the gathering of knowledge is not an end in itself. Neither is wisdom an end in itself. Scripture regards it as important that we properly use knowledge and wisdom we have acquired. Though discernment implies the ability to attain knowledge or gather data, more importantly, it suggests the ability to properly apply these. Proverbs 29:7 indicates as much where it says, "A righteous man knows the rights of the poor; a wicked man does not *understand* such knowledge." A person can have knowledge but still not truly understand it. He can have knowledge without discernment.

Those who attain wisdom are prepared to exercise discernment, a term we will now (finally!) define.

DISCERNMENT IN THE ORIGINAL LANGUAGES

The vast majority of the Bible was written in one of two languages: Hebrew or Greek. Each of these languages has a word that may be translated as "discernment." In Hebrew this word is *bin*. It appears almost 250 times in the Old Testament and is most commonly translated into English as "insight" or "understanding." It can mean to understand, consider, perceive, be prudent, or regard. Jay Adams notes that this word is related to a noun that means "interval" or "space between." "In essence it means to separate things from one another at their points of difference in order to distinguish them"[7] or "the process by which one comes to know or understand God's thoughts and ways through separating those things that differ." A note in the NET Bible says the term "refers to the ability to make distinctions between things. This is illustrated by its derivatives: The related preposition means 'between' and the related noun means 'space between.' So the verb refers to the ability to discern between moral options."[8]

The word *bin* has several relevant derivatives, namely *ben*, *bina*, and *tebuna*. I know that many readers are quickly bored by talk of the original biblical languages, but in this case I believe this discussion is crucial to our understanding of discernment, so hang in for just a few short paragraphs! I am confident that your efforts will be rewarded.

Space Between

Ben is generally translated as "between." It refers to intervals or spaces between objects. As it relates to discernment, it is used with verbs having to do with judging, knowing, or teaching where a

---

[7]Jay Adams, *A Call to Discernment* (Eugene, OR: Harvest House, 1987), 46.
[8]Note for Prov. 1:2.

person must distinguish between multiple options. We see this in 1 Kings 3:9, a verse we have already examined, where we read, "Give your servant therefore an understanding mind to govern your people, that I may discern *between* good and evil, for who is able to govern this your great people?" Isaiah 2:4 describes the Lord's act of judgment in which "he shall judge *between* the nations, and shall decide disputes for many peoples." In both these verses there are multiple options presented, and someone must examine the intervals between them, the differences apparent in them, and make a judgment about which is good or bad, right or wrong. We see, then, that the very basis of discernment is identifying differences and making judgments based on distinguishing between various options. Discernment is thinking in black-and-white terms, drawing clear lines between what is truth and error, what is good and evil.

Understanding

Bina is most commonly translated as "understanding," though it is also frequently rendered as "discerning." It refers to intellectual understanding, and even the very faculty of understanding. Proverbs 3:5 warns: "Do not lean on your own *understanding*." This is to say, do not lean on your own intellect or your own knowledge. One Bible dictionary says the word suggests "a good sense or wisdom to respond properly to the Lord and his Torah."[9] For example, in Daniel 10:1 we see the word used when Daniel was given the ability to understand a dream and to understand and explain its deepest meaning. *Bina* is the ability to understand the times (1 Chron. 12:32) and react well to decisions and situations faced in life.

Skill

Tebuna is also most commonly translated as "understanding." According to the same dictionary it implies cleverness, skill, or the capacity for discerning the right course of action (Deut. 32:28; Ps.

---

[9]James Swanson, *Dictionary of Biblical Languages with Semantic Domains: Hebrew (Old Testament)*, electronic ed. (Oak Harbor, WA: Logos Research Systems, 1997).

136:5; 147:5; Prov. 2:2; 3:19). It is sometimes related to skill with tools or implements, the common thread being "skill."[10]

Judging

The most common Greek word for discernment, *diakrino*, is very similar in meaning to the Hebrew. It also refers to separation and, besides "discernment," is also translated as "making . . . distinction" and "judged . . . truly." We can see how it is used in 1 Corinthians 2:14–15 where we encounter the word or its derivatives three times. "The natural person does not accept the things of the Spirit of God, for they are folly to him, and he is not able to understand them because they are spiritually *discerned*. The spiritual person *judges* all things, but is himself to be *judged* by no one."

These words and their derivatives help us close in on a definition for discernment. We have seen the concepts of separating, looking for differences, understanding the times, and exhibiting skill. Based on his studies one author says that discernment involves "skill in reaching understanding and knowledge by the use of a process of separation."[11] He also says discernment involves "the divinely given ability to distinguish God's thoughts and ways from all others."[12] This process of separation implies what we have already seen: that we must make judgments between right and wrong, truth and error. Discernment involves seeking points of difference and deciding which path veers towards error and which leads to truth. One of my favorite teachers, John MacArthur, affirms the importance of truth in discernment, defining it as "the ability to understand, interpret, and apply truth skillfully."[13]

Long study in the Bible led me to a definition that is structured around certain key words that seem critical to the emphases we find in Scripture: *skill, understand, apply, separate, truth, error, right, wrong.* I would encourage you to read the following definition two or three times. I have attempted not to waste any words, so pause if necessary on each word.

---

[10]James Swanson, *Dictionary of Biblical Languages with Semantic Domains.*
[11]Jay Adams, *A Call to Discernment,* 46.
[12]Ibid., 49.
[13]John MacArthur, *Reckless Faith: When the Church Loses Its Will to Discern* (Wheaton, IL: Crossway Books, 1994), *xv.*

Discernment is *the skill of understanding and applying God's Word with the purpose of separating truth from error and right from wrong.*

When we practice discernment, we are applying the truths of the Bible to our lives. We are attempting to understand the words of the Bible and trusting God's Word to give clarity so we might see things as God sees them. Our goal in discernment is to do just this: to see things through God's eyes through the Bible and thus to see things as they really are. Like wiping the steam from a mirror, we seek to remove what is opaque so we might see with God-given clarity.

To aid our understanding, we'll now briefly unpack this definition, looking at each of its individual components.

DISCERNMENT IS . . .

the Skill . . .

Discernment is a skill. It is not an inherent ability like breathing or chewing but a skill like reading or public speaking that must be practiced and must be improved. There is not a person on earth who has been born with a full measure of discernment or who has all of the discernment he will ever need. There is not a person who has attained a level of expertise that allows him to move on and to leave discernment behind. Like the master musician who practices his skills more as his acclaim grows, a discerning person will see with ever-greater clarity his need to increase in discernment. He will want to sharpen and improve this skill throughout his life.

God graciously enables and equips us to practice discernment with increasing accuracy and confidence. Like other skills, discernment increases with practice. An apprentice to a tailor will at first make slow, hesitant cuts to a piece of fabric. His experienced tutor, though, will confidently make accurate cuts in one smooth movement. In the same way, what is at first difficult can, with practice, become more natural. The more we know of truth, the more our ability to discern will increase.

While the Bible does not make it entirely clear, it is likely that God did not immediately bestow upon Solomon the full measure of his eventual wisdom and discernment. It is more likely that God gave Solomon ability but required that he continually sharpen this skill. After all, God also granted Solomon "both riches and honor," but these surely did not come in full measure that very day. Just as we are required to invest effort in learning what the Bible says and just as we are to strive after holiness, in the same way we are to work at the skill of discernment, attempting to become better at it through practice. This is clear from a verse we have already encountered several times. Hebrews 5:14 reads, "Solid food is for the mature, for those who have their powers of discernment trained by constant practice to distinguish good from evil." Distinguishing good from evil, and doing so correctly and consistently, requires dedicated, ongoing practice.

of understanding . . .

As we have just seen, the Hebrew word most commonly translated as "discernment" is otherwise translated as "understanding." Discernment is closely related to understanding and depends upon rightly and accurately knowing God and his ways. Because we can only base what we do on what we know, we must first understand who God is and how he wants us to serve and honor him. Understanding must precede both interpretation and application. This is clear throughout the Bible, but especially in Proverbs where Solomon continually ties knowledge, wisdom, and discernment, not as separate disciplines, but as related. And so to be people of discernment we must be people who dedicate ourselves to studying, knowing, and understanding God.

and applying . . .

Discernment involves not only understanding but the application of that understanding. This is where we see the interrelated nature of wisdom and discernment, and where we see how difficult it can be to separate one from the other. Discernment is wisdom in action, wisdom applied, and here we seek to apply the skill we have been practicing. We not only know (understand), but we also do (apply).

God's Word . . .

God's Word refers to two aspects of God's revelation: revelation of himself through the person of Jesus Christ and revelation of himself through speech, and in particular, the words that have been recorded in the Bible. Though in days past God revealed himself through words of prophecy and other forms of personal address, today we know him primarily through the Bible, which has been given to point us to the Word of God as it exists in the person of Jesus.[14]

God's Word is truth. In John 17:17, as part of his High Priestly Prayer, Jesus prayed to his Father, "your word is truth." God's Word is the very source of infallible truth. God's Word is our measure; it is our source. Hebrews 5:13 says that "everyone who lives on milk is unskilled in the word of righteousness, since he is a child." Conversely, then, those who are mature must be those who are skilled in the word of righteousness. The word of righteousness, those doctrines that are fundamental to the Christian faith, are synonymous with the Word of God.

We can only worship and glorify God on the basis of what we know of him. In order to be discerning, we must know and understand what is true about God. To do this we turn to God's Word. And so, to be discerning, we must first be students of the Bible. We must study it, we must read about it, and we must hear it taught from the pulpit. This is the purpose of Psalm 119, the longest psalm in the Bible and one that dwells constantly upon God's Word. The author turns continually to the Scripture as his source of discernment. In verse 66 he writes, "Teach me good judgment [discernment] and knowledge, for I believe in your commandments." Then, "Through your precepts I get understanding [discernment]; therefore I hate every false way," he says (v. 104). And in verse 100 he speaks of the discernment he has already been given, stating, "I understand more than the aged, for I keep your precepts." He is more discerning than those who are older than he is because he has studied, understood, and kept God's law as revealed in Scripture. John MacArthur writes:

---

[14]Wayne Grudem, *Systematic Theology: An Introduction to Biblical Doctrine* (Leicester: Inter-Varsity Press, 1994), 50.

Discernment intersects the Christian life at every point. And God's Word provides us with the needed discernment about every issue of life. According to Peter, God *"has granted to us everything pertaining to life and godliness, through the true knowledge of Him who called us by His own glory and excellence"* (2 Peter 1:3). You see, it is through the *"true knowledge of Him,"* that we have been given everything we need to live a Christian life in this fallen world. And how else do we have true knowledge of God but through the pages of His Word, the Bible? In fact, Peter goes on to say that such knowledge comes through God's granting *"to us His precious and magnificent promises"* (2 Peter 1:4).[15]

When we engage in discernment we attempt to use God's Word to rise above our own limitations so we can see as God sees. Through the truths contained in the Bible, God allows us to see things with his eyes. We look to his Word, our guide to all matters of life and faith, and learn how to serve and honor him.

with the purpose of separating . . .

God's Word is the standard we use to differentiate between what is true and what is false. We have seen that the concepts of *separating* and *distinguishing* are inherent in the words from the original languages that we have translated as "discernment." Discernment implies, as we have already seen, that we are to separate things in order to understand their differences.

Like the laser level that shows with perfect clarity any deviations from what is straight, the Bible teaches what is true, leaving what is false standing out with glaring clearness. We use God's Word as a tool to separate what is true from what is false. We use it to make the light appear lighter, leaving the dark to appear ever darker.

truth from error . . .

A constant theme when discussing spiritual discernment is the importance of distinguishing truth from error. The Bible makes it clear that doctrine is either true or false. We are called by God to

---

[15]John MacArthur, "What Is Biblical Discernment and Why Is it Important?" (http://www.ondoctrine.com/ 2gty0301.htm) (emphasis in original).

examine all theology and to make such binary distinctions. When we speak of truth and error we speak of doctrine and theology—ways of thinking rightly and truly about God. We think about how we think, knowing that what we think inevitably affects how we act. What we think of God will necessarily impact how we serve him. If we want to serve him in a way that is true and pure, we must think of him as he really is, thinking of him without error. Only when we have separated truth from error are we able to rightly worship God.

and right from wrong.

At times discernment will be concerned with truth and error. At other times it will be concerned with *right* and *wrong*, words that indicate a moral dimension to discernment, for this practice concerns itself not only with doctrine and theology, but with the practical application of those disciplines to our lives. Discernment is a skill we need to live lives that are morally and ethically pleasing to God. We need to be discerning first in what we believe and then in what we do. Whereas the concepts of truth and error concern what we believe, the associated concepts of right and wrong concern what we do and how we live. In this way we see discernment as a discipline that applies to all areas of life.

FURTHER DEFINING

To aid our understanding, we'll turn now to several other important aspects of discernment.

The Source

Spiritual discernment is a gift from God (which is not necessarily to say that it is a spiritual gift, a topic we will examine in greater detail in a later chapter). We see this most clearly in Scripture in the story of Solomon and the request he made of God. "Give your servant therefore an understanding mind to govern your people, that I may discern between good and evil, for who is able to govern this your great people?" (1 Kings 3:9). Solomon asked for wisdom, and it was given to him as a gracious gift from God. He then wrote and compiled many proverbs, the purpose of which is:

> To know wisdom and instruction,
> > to understand words of insight [discernment],
> to receive instruction in wise dealing,
> > in righteousness, justice, and equity;
> to give prudence to the simple,
> > knowledge and discretion to the youth. (Prov. 1:2–4)

Solomon, aware of his own inadequacies and aware that God is the very source of all good gifts, asked God for discernment, and this ability was granted to him. God is ready, willing, and able to bestow this gift upon others who ask for it. After all, "which one of you, if his son asks him for bread, will give him a stone?" (Matt. 7:9). He is pleased to give to his children that which they request, provided those requests bring honor and glory to him. James, the brother of Jesus, encouraged his readers to seek wisdom: "If any of you lacks wisdom, let him ask God, who gives generously to all without reproach, and it will be given him" (James 1:5).

In 1 Corinthians 2:14–15 Paul writes, "The natural person does not accept the things of the Spirit of God, for they are folly to him, and he is not able to understand them because they are spiritually discerned. The spiritual person judges all things, but is himself to be judged by no one." The natural person, the person who has not been saved, is unable to understand the things of the Spirit—the teachings of Scripture. People who do not have the Spirit cannot be discerning.

The Power

Spiritual discernment is not only an ability that has God as its source, but it is an ability that is continually empowered by God. God does not simply hand us the fully formed skill of discernment and leave us to our own devices. Rather, he gives us the Holy Spirit to indwell us and to assist us as we encounter truth and error. It is only through the ongoing, moment-by-moment ministry of the Holy Spirit that we can exercise discernment. Solomon writes:

> For the Lord gives wisdom;
>   from his mouth come knowledge and understanding;
> he stores up sound wisdom for the upright;
>   he is a shield to those who walk in integrity,
> guarding the paths of justice
>   and watching over the way of his saints. (Prov. 2:6–8)

The apostle Paul writes of this as well:

> For who knows a person's thoughts except the spirit of that person, which is in him? So also no one comprehends the thoughts of God except the Spirit of God. Now we have received not the spirit of the world, but the Spirit who is from God, that we might understand the things freely given us by God. And we impart this in words not taught by human wisdom but taught by the Spirit, interpreting spiritual truths to those who are spiritual. The natural person does not accept the things of the Spirit of God, for they are folly to him, and he is not able to understand them because they are spiritually discerned. (1 Cor. 2:11–14)

Only those who are indwelt by the Holy Spirit have the capacity to exercise true spiritual discernment. Without the Holy Spirit—without spiritual discernment—Christians would be no better off than unbelievers, for we would stumble blindly in our search for truth, never being able to separate truth from error.

The Process

While the source of discernment is the Holy Spirit, and while the power of discernment is God, it is still a process and something we must work at. Though at times the process may seem immediate, more often we will need to think carefully about how to distinguish or separate truth from error and right from wrong. A later chapter will narrow in on this part of the definition and teach a process you can use to practice discernment. For now, it is sufficient to know that, with our understanding of the truth, we must exercise dedicated and deliberate effort in distinguishing between what is true and what is false.

The Heart and the Head

Some Christians have been taught that discernment is a matter of the heart more than a matter of the head. They teach that discernment is an intuitive or subjective matter of the Spirit working through the heart rather than an objective, intellectual matter of using the mind to test, weigh, and judge. They may level criticism at those who discern with the mind rather than with the heart. For these people, a matter that is decided by reason and rationality may seem to be a matter that bypasses the Holy Spirit. Christian apologist Gregory Koukl has often been faced with this question.

> "Koukl, you're just in your head too much," they suggest. "You're too left-brained when it comes to spiritual things. You're too logical, too reasonable. You don't depend enough on your heart to discern the spiritual realm. Yes you're using your mind, but what about your spirit? Why do you always trust in your own thinking instead of what the Spirit is saying about something?"
>
> These statements imply that somehow I'm not doing a full-blooded assessment of things because I'm only using half of my machinery. My analysis should include the subjective, not just the objective.[16]

There are two concerns with this critique. First, it implies that there are two levels of discernment, one that is purely rational and depends on the mind, and another that is subjective and depends on the heart or on feelings. Second, it implies that this second level of discernment is superior to the first and somehow relies more fully upon the Holy Spirit. It supposedly moves beyond the limited mental capabilities of humans and allows the Spirit to interact directly with the heart of the believer to notify him of some problem or some error.

Of greater concern is the fact that the understanding of two levels of discernment, one objective and one subjective, cannot be supported by the Bible. A survey of passages of Scripture relevant to the subject of discernment, words dealing with testing, judging,

---

[16]Greg Koukl, "Discernment: Head or Heart?" (http://www.str.org/site/News2?page=News Article&id= 5204).

approving, and the like, will reveal nothing that would allow us to believe that the Holy Spirit will provide some type of subjective sense of discernment apart from the Bible. Instead we see that discernment points us continually to the Scriptures, to the objective source of truth meant to guide us in all matters of life and faith. Any method that points anywhere but Scripture implicitly points *away* from Scripture. It must be rejected.

Writing on this subject, John MacArthur says, "Biblical faith . . . is rational. It is reasonable. It is intelligent. It makes good sense. And spiritual truth is meant to be rationally contemplated, examined logically, studied, analyzed, and employed as the only reliable basis for making wise judgments. That process is precisely what Scripture calls *discernment*."[17] Like MacArthur, Koukl concludes, "When the Bible talks about discernment—when it talks about assessing spiritual things—it's talking about a rational assessment based on objective criterion. You can't be 'too much in your head' when it comes to spiritual discernment. Using your head is spiritual discernment, if you're using the truth properly."[18] Spiritual discernment is a pursuit that must always engage the mind. We discern truth from error and right from wrong by using our minds to search Scripture, to recall Scripture, and to compare everything to Scripture. Without the Bible and its objective truths there can be no discernment.

Scripture repeatedly shows this correlation between discernment and knowledge, between discernment and a mind that is saturated with and shaped by the Bible. In Psalm 119:66 the psalmist writes, "Teach me good judgment and knowledge, for I believe in your commandments." The words translated "good judgment" could as easily be translated "discernment" and, indeed, are rendered that way in certain translations.[19] Philippians 1:9 says similarly, "And it is my prayer that your love may abound more and more, with knowledge and all discernment." And again in Proverbs 16:21 we read, "The wise of heart is called discerning," and in Proverbs 15:14, "The heart of him who has understanding [the discerning person] seeks knowledge, but the mouths of fools feed on folly."

---

[17]John MacArthur, *Reckless Faith*, xvi (emphasis in original).
[18]Greg Koukl, "Discernment: Head or Heart?"
[19]The *New American Standard Bible* (NASB) and *The NET Bible* (NET) both use "discernment."

The evidence continues to mount in Proverbs 18:15 where we read, "The discerning person acquires knowledge" (NET), and Proverbs 19:25, which says, "Strike a scoffer, and the simple will learn prudence; reprove a man of understanding [a discerning man], and he will gain knowledge." The testimony of Scripture is plain: while spiritual discernment is a practice that is absolutely dependent upon the work of the Holy Spirit, God has so ordained that it is also a discipline that relies on the mind.

The Purpose

The purpose of discernment is to further the chief end of man, the foremost reason we exist, which, to borrow the words of the Westminster Shorter Catechism, is "to glorify God and to enjoy him forever."[20] By being people of discernment, we bring glory to God and learn to enjoy him ever and ever more. Conversely, if we refuse to exercise discernment and are swayed by every wind of doctrine, we deny him the glory that is rightly his and do not learn to enjoy him more.

The End

We will not always need to exercise discernment. Discernment is a discipline necessary only in a world in which we are faced with sin and temptation. When God created Adam and Eve, he made them sinless and yet with the ability to choose between good and evil. Tragically, they displayed poor discernment, falling for the wiles of the Devil and bringing sin into the world. We live now between the beginning and the end, and, though it is now impossible for us to go through life without sinning, we make decisions moment-by-moment and day-by-day in which we use discernment to attempt to separate what is right from what is wrong and what is true from what is false so that we can bring glory and honor to God. But when Jesus Christ returns and this world passes away, the need for discernment will also pass away. In heaven we will no longer be able to sin. There will be no error, no wrong for us to fall prey to. We will no longer need to be discerning and will no longer have to test

---

[20]Westminster Shorter Catechism, Question and Answer 1.

and try what we do and what we believe. Discernment is a process that prepares us for heaven and enables us to eagerly await the end of discernment.

Thus we see that discernment begins and ends with God. God provides the ability to know him and to make decisions that please him so that we may serve him and bring glory to his name. Biblical discernment is always, ever, and innately a spiritual task.

To think biblically about life, we must be willing and able to make clear distinctions between God's ways and all other ways. We must be willing to think deeply about issues and to dedicate time and effort to learning what is right and what is wrong. We must also be willing to grow in our knowledge of God and of the Bible, for this is where we will learn of God's ways.

KEY THOUGHT

Discernment is the skill of understanding and applying God's Word with the purpose of separating truth from error and right from wrong. It is a task in which we attempt to see things as God sees them. People who are discerning have a heightened ability to see and understand issues from God's perspective. Empowered by his Spirit, they strive for and are given an understanding of what is pleasing to God and what is not. They do this by understanding God through his Word, the Bible, and by applying the wisdom of the Bible to their lives. All the while it is God who gives the motivation, the desire, the ability, and the power to both know and discern.

chapter four

the HEART of DISCERNMENT

Test everything; hold fast what is good.
Abstain from every form of evil.

1 THESSALONIANS 5:21-22

A SHORT TIME AGO I SAW a gag show on television in which a comedy troupe set up shop in a small corner store. One woman played the part of the storekeeper, standing behind the counter and ringing up sales. Another member of the team pretended to be a blind man. He stumbled around the store, his eyes hidden behind dark sunglasses. He eventually asked the shopkeeper for an item and handed her a twenty-dollar bill. The shopkeeper took the money, looked around furtively, and hastily gathered a few bill-sized pieces of blank paper. Pretending that this was his change, she handed these to the blind man and sent him on his way. Innocent bystanders were aghast and tried to convince the blind man that he had been taken advantage of. They tried to pull the phony money from his hands and to scold the dishonest shopkeeper. And then, as happens with all of these gag shows, it was revealed that there were hidden cameras throughout the store and that the bystanders had been the butt of a coordinated joke.

This is a funny sketch (though not quite as funny as the one where they somehow manage to swap an innocent person's poodle for a massive Saint Bernard) but one that made me think (after I had finished laughing). You see, several months ago I sat in the offices of the Bank of Canada, the organization responsible for printing and maintaining Canada's money, and experienced a moment that tested my humility. An expert on counterfeit currency asked me whether I always verify that the currency I am given, whether in a bank or a store, is genuine. I was asked in such a way that the expected answer was "of course I do!" And yet I had to admit that I had never considered the importance of verifying the validity of the money given to me.

Furthermore, I was uncertain that I would even know what to look for. It seems so obvious—of course I should check my money!—yet I had so often overlooked this simple test. I may as well have been that blind man accepting worthless slips of blank paper. I learned that day that I understand the importance of discernment in some areas and practice discernment in some areas, but I do not in others.

When we defined *discernment* in the last chapter, we reached the unavoidable conclusion that discerning is closely related to judging. As we discern between what is good and evil and between what is right and wrong we necessarily make judgments. We weigh evidence in the balance and decide what represents truth and what represents falsehood. But judging is not popular in our culture. The phrase "Don't judge me!" is seen as an inviolable mantra in this postmodern society. We live in a culture that values autonomy to the point of irrationality. We live in a culture that teaches we can and should do whatever makes us happy and that no one has the right to hold us up to any standard but our own. Judging is the great sin of postmodernism.

Of course, Jesus himself taught that judgment is wrong:

> Judge not, that you be not judged. For with the judgment you pronounce you will be judged, and with the measure you use it will be measured to you. Why do you see the speck that is in your brother's eye, but do not notice the log that is in your own eye? Or

how can you say to your brother, "Let me take the speck out of your eye," when there is the log in your own eye? You hypocrite, first take the log out of your own eye, and then you will see clearly to take the speck out of your brother's eye. (Matt. 7:1–5)

And yet, as we saw in the verse at the beginning of this chapter, the Bible also makes it clear that we are to "test all things." So what are we to do? Are we to judge or are we not to judge?

CAN WE JUDGE?

There are some parts of the Bible that seem to contradict other parts. Many books have been published that claim to list the Bible's contradictions, offering proof that the Bible cannot be anything other than a flawed human invention. A great many Christians have invested a great deal of time in explaining how things that appear contradictory can in fact be reconciled. And under even cursory examination, each of these so-called contradictions is shown not to be contradictory at all. J. I. Packer, in his classic book *Evangelism and the Sovereignty of God*, discusses *antinomy*, a word he defines as "an appearance of contradiction between conclusions which seem equally logical, reasonable or necessary."[1] We see *antinomy* often in the Scriptures. For example, we know that God has given human beings a measure of freedom, some kind of free will. At the same time, though, we see in the Bible that God claims absolute supremacy and sovereignty over the world and all that happens in it. The same God who claims to predestine some to eternal life calls all to turn and to make a decision to accept him. The God who hardened the heart of Pharaoh is the same God who holds Pharaoh responsible for his sin. Are these contradictory, or can they be reconciled? Is this contradiction or is it antinomy?

If we believe that God is the author of the Bible, and that God always and only speaks the truth, we must believe that the Bible never truly contradicts itself. Rather than declaring the existence of a contradiction, we need to seek to understand how two conclusions can be reconciled.

---

[1] J. I. Packer, *Evangelism and the Sovereignty of God* (Downers Grove, IL: InterVarsity), 18.

Jesus' words that were quoted earlier are probably the ones he is best known for: "Judge not, that you be not judged" (Matt. 7:1). Even unbelievers, who refuse to accept almost all that Jesus taught, often take refuge in these words. From these words alone we could conclude that we are commanded never to judge anyone or anything. And yet the apostle Paul, writing under the inspiration of the Holy Spirit, states, "Test everything; hold fast what is good. Abstain from every form of evil" (1 Thess. 5:21–22). John, writing decades after the death of Jesus, wrote, "Beloved, do not believe every spirit, but test the spirits to see whether they are from God, for many false prophets have gone out into the world" (1 John 4:1). From these passages it seems clear that we *are* to judge, and we are to judge everything. It seems from some portions of the Bible that we are told not to judge and yet in others we are told to judge everything. And so, in our quest to understand spiritual discernment, we will first seek to understand what and how we are to judge.

The stakes are high. In his book *Who Are You to Judge?* Dave Swavely makes the astute observation that "the sin of judging is a root cause in most of the interpersonal conflicts that arise in the lives of believers, and so learning to identify and avoid this sin will go a long way toward promoting peace and joy in the body of Christ."[2] Matthew Henry agrees, writing, "Judging rightly concerning men, and not judging more highly of them than is fit, is one way to prevent quarrels and contentions in the churches. Pride commonly lies at the bottom of these quarrels."[3] At the same time, the sin of not judging, of not exercising discernment, is a root cause in the breakdown of many formerly godly churches and organizations. To never judge is to open the church to all manner of spiritual evil and deception.

So what about the Bible—does it tell us that we may not judge at all? Or does it tell us otherwise? By examining the many passages dealing with discerning, judging, and testing, we soon find that not all judging is equal. There are times when we may and must judge and times when we may not and must not judge.

---

[2]Dave Swavely, *Who Are You to Judge?* (Phillipsburg, NJ: P&R, 2005), 2.
[3]Matthew Henry, *Matthew Henry's Commentary on the Whole Bible: Complete and Unabridged in One Volume* (Peabody, MA: Hendrickson, 1996).

WHAT WE MUST NOT JUDGE

There are two broad categories in which judgment is sinful and forbidden by God.

1) Going beyond What Is Written

The first kind of sinful judging is that of hypocritical judging or judging people on the basis of what is hidden to us.

> But with me it is a very small thing that I should be judged by you or by any human court. In fact, I do not even judge myself. I am not aware of anything against myself, but I am not thereby acquitted. It is the Lord who judges me. Therefore do not pronounce judgment before the time, before the Lord comes, who will bring to light the things now hidden in darkness and will disclose the purposes of the heart. Then each one will receive his commendation from God.
>
> I have applied all these things to myself and Apollos for your benefit, brothers, that you may learn by us not to go beyond what is written, that none of you may be puffed up in favor of one against another. For who sees anything different in you? What do you have that you did not receive? If then you received it, why do you boast as if you did not receive it? (1 Cor. 4:3–7)

In this passage Paul exhorts the church at Corinth not to judge one another, yet he refers to a specific kind of judgment. He provides several conditions. First, he puts a limit on the time, saying that we are not to judge "before the Lord comes." Second, we are not to judge "beyond what is written." This shows that there is an objective standard by which we may judge, but that we cannot proceed further than this standard. The standard, of course, is the Bible. We may judge doctrine and behavior by the objective standards of right and wrong that are given to us in Scripture. What we may not do, though, is judge a person's heart and motives.

The members of the church of Corinth, it seems, were habitually evaluating their leaders, judging who was superior and placing themselves under those people. In so doing they were bringing division to their local church. Paul's letter warns them to withhold judgment, for, he says, they are unable to make accurate judgments. The limits of human knowledge, the ability to see only the outside rather than the heart, means that humans are incapable of accurate judgments about matters of the heart and conscience. Paul uses himself as a model, stating that he refuses to worry a great deal about how others judge him. In fact, Paul states that he will not even judge himself on these matters, for his limited knowledge prevents him from seeing into the deep recesses of even his own heart. He has examined his life and is not aware of anything that would qualify as ongoing sin. And so he leaves the rest up to God and awaits the day of judgment where all will be made clear. If we are unable to even fully understand our own hearts, how much less are we capable of passing judgment on the hearts of others?

And so we are to ensure we do not "pronounce judgment before the time." This does not refer to all judgments, for Paul affirms that he has examined himself. Rather, we are not to pronounce judgment on the matters we cannot see, know, or properly evaluate. We are not to judge motives or the righteousness of other believers.

2) Matters of Conscience

There is another area we may not judge.

> As for the one who is weak in faith, welcome him, but not to quarrel over opinions. One person believes he may eat anything, while the weak person eats only vegetables. Let not the one who eats despise the one who abstains, and let not the one who abstains pass judgment on the one who eats, for God has welcomed him. Who are you to pass judgment on the servant of another? It is before his own master that he stands or falls. And he will be upheld, for the Lord is able to make him stand. (Rom. 14:1–4)

Just as we may not judge motives and personal piety, we may not judge matters of conscience where the Bible offers no explicit directive. Each of us, individually, is a servant of Christ, and we must stand firm in what we feel our Master demands of us based on our studies of the Bible. In so doing we will be upheld by the Lord. The power of Christ will provide the steadfast power needed to remain strong. Writing about matters we must not judge, Matthew Henry writes:

> It is judging out of season, and judging at an adventure. [Paul] is not to be understood of judging by persons in authority, within the verge of their office, nor of private judging concerning facts that are notorious; but of judging persons' future state, or the secret springs and principles of their actions, or about facts doubtful in themselves. To judge in these cases, and give decisive sentence, is to assume the seat of God and challenge his prerogative. Note, How bold a sinner is the forward and severe censurer! How ill-timed and arrogant are his censures! But there is one who will judge the censurer, and those he censures, without prejudice, passion, or partiality. And there is a time coming when men cannot fail judging aright concerning themselves and others, by following his judgment. This should make them now cautious of judging others, and careful in judging themselves.[4]

We have seen, then, that there are certain things we should not and thus cannot judge. We cannot pass judgment on matters that are hidden in darkness. We cannot judge motives, we cannot judge personal piety, and we cannot judge the conscience in matters where Scripture is silent. Were we to do these things, we would be guilty of legalism, sinful judging systematized, or "creating moral standards beyond what the Scripture has revealed."[5]

Were we to judge on the basis of what is hidden to us, we would be guilty of sinful judging. Swavely defines sinful judging as "negatively evaluating someone's conduct or spiritual state on the basis of nonbiblical standards or suspected motives."[6] Said more colloquially, to judge others is to decide that they are doing wrong because they do something the Bible doesn't talk about or because you think you can guess what is in that person's heart.[7]

We have seen what we may not and must not judge: things that are hidden to us—hidden by our sinful pride or hidden by our

---

[4]Matthew Henry, *Matthew Henry's Commentary on the Whole Bible.*
[5]Dave Swavely, *Who Are You to Judge?* 55.
[6]Ibid., 8.
[7]Ibid.

human limitations. And now we rightly ask what things we may and must judge.

WHAT WE MUST JUDGE

The Bank of Canada has tried to educate the Canadian population with a short and simple mantra: "touch, tilt, look at, look through." These words refer to four simple tests that can be done quickly and easily and can immediately show a bill to be genuine or counterfeit. There may be some circumstances when one or more of the tests are not possible, such as the "look through" test in a darkened room, but it should always be possible to perform at least a couple of them. It is wise to test currency, for as I was reminded time and again during my visit to the Bank of Canada, once I have accepted a piece of currency, I am responsible for it. If I accept a counterfeit hundred-dollar bill and attempt to deposit it at the bank, the bill will be taken from me and destroyed, leaving me one hundred dollars poorer! The stakes are high. Thankfully, I have a legal right to reject any piece of currency that is given to me and to request a replacement. If I make a purchase in a store and am handed a bill that I feel is fraudulent, I can return that bill and request another one. The bill does not become my responsibility until I have accepted it and have taken possession of it.

The same is true when it comes to spiritual discernment. When a doctrine or teaching is presented to me, I may examine it and mull it over. I may compare it to Scripture and seek to understand whether it is consistent with what God has revealed about himself. But once I accept that doctrine I am responsible for it. If the doctrine is false and I choose to believe it, I can expect God to hold me accountable for believing something that is false. "Blessed is the one who has no reason to pass judgment on himself for what he approves," says Paul (Rom. 14:22). And so I must exercise great caution and great care in ensuring that I accept and approve only that which the Bible teaches. I need to test everything that is presented to me. I cannot be like the blind man I spoke of at the beginning of this chapter.

Like separating genuine from counterfeit currency, the practice of discernment is simple. It involves only a single test that will nec-essarily evoke one of two responses: action or response—that is all. First Thessalonians 5:21–22 describes the test and the possible reac-tions: "Test everything; hold fast what is good. Abstain from every form of evil." First, we take action by testing to determine whether something is consistent with Scripture. Having done that, we take one of two actions: we either abstain from what is evil and coun-terfeit, or we hold fast to what is genuine and good. We reject what is error and embrace what is truth. We turn away from what is bad and turn towards what is good. We will dedicate a whole chapter to understanding what it means to hold fast to what is good and to abstain from every form of evil. But first we need to understand what the Bible means by "test everything."

TEST EVERYTHING

Test

The word translated as "test" is from the common Greek word *dokimazo,* the root of which can also mean *prove, try, examine,* or *discern.* It points toward a process of testing or validating in order to prove that something is genuine. Donald Barnhouse tells how this word was used in ancient times:

> In the ancient world there was no banking system as we know it today, and no paper money. All money was made from metal heated until liquid, poured into moulds, and allowed to cool. When the coins were cool, it was necessary to smooth off the uneven edges. The coins were comparatively soft, and of course many people shaved them closely. In one century, more than eighty laws were passed in Athens to stop the practice of shaving down the coins then in circulation. But some money changers were men of integrity, who would accept no counterfeit money; they were men of honor who put only genuine, full-weight money into cir-culation. Such men were called *dokimos* or *approved.*[8]

To understand this, we must realize that ancient economies dif-fered from modern ones in that coins had inherent value. The value

---

[8]Donald Grey Barnhouse, *Romans: God's Glory* (Grand Rapids, MI Eerdmans, 1964), 18.

of a coin was related to the metal from which it was made and the weight of that metal. Today our coins are typically worth far less than their component parts but have a value assigned to them. In ancient times a coin was worth its weight in gold or whatever other metal it was made from. So when a person shaved a coin, he was deviously reducing the value of that coin. He would collect the pieces he shaved off and soon have a quantity of gold that he could sell. While many people would shave down the coins, removing small flecks of the precious metals and then passing along the coins which were now reduced in value, some wise and honest men refused to do this, and they were the ones who had been tested and approved. They were men of honor and integrity.

We are to be discerning about all things and are to ensure we only believe what has been approved. We are to test all things, discerning between what pleases the Lord and what does not. This is the right and responsibility of each Christian, and we must do this both as churches and as individuals. We cannot rely on others to be discerning on our behalf. We cannot depend on others to do this work for us. Rather, as we saw in "A Call to Discernment" at the beginning of this book, discernment is the responsibility of each Christian. Such is the right and privilege of Protestants, those who believe that we need no infallible mediator of truth other than the Bible. We do not turn to another human authority to discern for us, but we look prayerfully to Scripture, trusting the Holy Spirit to fill us and to guide us.

Everything

The Bible can seem a little bit confusing when it comes to words like *all* or *everyone* or *everything*. There is one little Greek word *pas* that has a whole array of meanings and is variously translated as "all," "all things," "everyone," "all men," "whosoever," "whatsoever." There are times when this word points toward situations that are contextual and times that point toward situations that are universal. We might also say that there are times when this word indicates "all without exception" and others where it indicates "all without distinction." In John 12:19 the Pharisees say of Jesus, "Look, the world has gone after him." Of course they did not mean that every person in every part of the world had gone after Jesus. Rather, they were indicating that a great number of people within a certain context were following after him. They were indicating that all kinds of people (or all without distinction) had gone after him, and that so many people were following the Lord that it may well have *seemed* as if the whole world was going after him. Of course, there are other times where the Bible really does refer to all people in a universal sense. When Luke quotes Paul saying, "The times of ignorance God overlooked, but now he commands all people everywhere to repent" (Acts 17:30), he means that God commands repentance of all people, everywhere, and in all times. He extends this outward call to all without exception.

So which is the "all things" or "everything" we encounter in 1 Thessalonians 5:21? Is it universal or is there some context we need to understand? It seems clear from Scripture that spiritual discernment applies to spiritual matters—matters of life and faith. When we are commanded to test everything, we are told to test and prove all that is relevant to the Christian life and faith. So what are these matters of life and faith? To at least some extent, everything relates to life and faith! We should not be Christians who compartmentalize our lives so that some areas are given over to the lordship of Christ and others are held back for ourselves. We cannot have components of our lives that are religious while others are secular. Christians with a truly Christian worldview will know that all of life is to be lived in accordance with biblical principles. Everything we do—whether it is choosing a church, reading a book, watching television, engaging in evangelism, forming friendships, studying the Bible—everything requires discernment. Because there is no area in which we have perfect understanding, there is no area of life that is beyond our need or ability to be discerning.

Yet while we are to test everything, this does not indicate that we are to *try* everything. Children try everything. You have seen it and I have seen it. As I mentioned in an earlier chapter, I have a vivid memory seared into my brain from when my son was just a couple of years old. I brought him downstairs one morning and sat him on the floor while I went off to fetch a glass of juice. I came back just a few seconds later and saw him still sitting near where I had left him moments before, but he was now holding a spoon that he must have found lying on the ground. His jaw was moving up and down. I hurried over to see what it was that he had found and put into his mouth. I still feel sick when I think about it. That is all you'll get out of me, but suffice it to say that it was something absolutely ghastly that is in no way fit for human consumption! Ever! But being a child he saw something on the floor and just had to try it. He had to chew it to see what it was.

The requirement to test all things does not mandate that, like children, we are to attempt everything once. We do not necessarily need to touch or experience things to know that they are evil. Abstaining from evil does not give us a lot of leeway to play with the doctrine, to tinker with it, and to try it out. If it is wrong, we are to shun it, to throw it away, and even to flee from it. We should exercise great caution in dealing with such doctrines, always keeping in mind our sinful tendencies to become attracted to and enamored with such doctrines (remember Frodo and his evil ring!). I wish I could have told my son that what he tasted was not meant to be eaten (a lesson he learned rather more disgustingly, unfortunately). He could have asked and I would have told him. And yet we, as full-grown men and women, often do not act a whole lot better. Like children, we often feel we need to sample things before we can determine if they are good or bad, truth or error. But God tells us we are to test, not sample. We need only compare things to the Word of God, the unchangeable and objective standard of right and wrong, truth and error. We can save ourselves all manner of pain and evil by simply going straight to the Bible.

So while we do not need to try everything, we do need to test everything—everything that is relevant to the Christian life. "Test everything": these simple words provide a filter through which everything must pass. All through the New Testament we see Christians testing, proving, and approving. All manner of matters of life and faith are tested. Any teaching to which we are introduced is to be tested. Any decision we face is to be tested. There should be no belief, no teaching, no action in the life of the Christian or in the church that has not been thoroughly tested or scrutinized. The Bible provides many examples of those who tested. Here are some of the areas that the Bible teaches we need to test.

Teaching

The members of the church at Berea are commended in the Bible for testing the words of Paul and Silas to ensure that they were consistent with the Scriptures of the Old Testament. "Now these Jews were more noble than those in Thessalonica; they received the word with all eagerness, examining the Scriptures daily to see if these things were so" (Acts 17:11).

Prophecy

The immediate context of 1 Thessalonians 5:20–21 teaches that prophecy is to be tested. "Do not despise prophecies, but test everything" (1 Thess. 5:20–21a).

Spirits

We are to test spirits to determine if they are the spirits sent from God or from Satan. "Beloved, do not believe every spirit, but test the spirits to see whether they are from God, for many false prophets have gone out into the world" (1 John 4:1).

Leaders

Those who are suited to serve as leaders in the church must first be tested and proven. Under the church's examination they must demonstrate conduct that is consistent with their profession of faith. "Let them also be tested first; then let them serve as deacons if they prove themselves blameless" (1 Tim. 3:10).

Other Believers

When Paul sent Titus and two other godly men to minister to the church in Corinth, he felt it necessary to indicate that he and his fellow apostles had tested an unnamed disciple and had found him suitable to serve among them in the local church. "And with them we are sending our brother whom we have often tested and found earnest in many matters, but who is now more earnest than ever because of his great confidence in you" (2 Cor. 8:22).

The Times

Jesus criticized a crowd of his followers for their inability to properly understand the times and for not properly discerning who Jesus was and what he had come to do. "You know how to interpret the appearance of earth and sky, but why do you not know how to interpret the present time?" (Luke 12:56)

Ourselves

The Bible often emphasizes the importance of personal testing and examination. For example, we are to test ourselves to see that we are truly saved. Testing will show whether we have the characteristics of those who call themselves followers of the Lord Jesus. "Examine yourselves, to see whether you are in the faith. Test yourselves. Or do you not realize this about yourselves, that Jesus Christ is in you?— unless indeed you fail to meet the test!" (2 Cor. 13:5). Even if we are confident that we are saved, we are to ensure that we are living in a way consistent with our profession. Paul exhorts young Timothy to "do your best to present yourself to God as one approved" (2 Tim. 2:15a). There are also occasions where we are to put ourselves through a time of special testing, for when discussing the celebration of the Lord's Supper, Paul says, "Let a person examine himself, then, and so eat of the bread and drink of the cup" (1 Cor. 11:28).

In short, we are to test everything! Everything that relates to Christian life and spirituality is to be thoroughly tested and approved. Nothing is excluded.

PRIORITIES

Though we are to test everything, there are some areas of Christian life and doctrine that are of greater consequence than others. Dr. Albert Mohler, reflecting on a visit to the emergency room of a local hospital, speaks of the need for "theological triage." In the medical field triage is a system of quickly classifying and prioritizing patients on the basis of the severity of their conditions, ensuring that those with the most severe illnesses or injuries are given the fastest and most thorough treatment. The success of this system depends upon the expertise of the medical experts who must be available to make quick and accurate assessments and decisions. Mohler writes:

> Today's Christian faces the daunting task of strategizing which Christian doctrines and theological issues are to be given highest priority in terms of our contemporary context. This applies both to the public defense of Christianity in face of the secular challenge and the internal responsibility of dealing with doctrinal disagreements.[9]

While all of God's truth is important and worth defending (just as each patient in a hospital is important and requires treatment), we must decide which issues deserve the greatest and most immediate attention in our efforts to be discerning. Just as it would make little sense to treat a man with a broken finger before treating one with a gunshot wound to the chest, it would make little sense to make the focus of our discernment issues that are disputable matters, all the while ignoring issues that are of far greater consequence.

Mohler proposes three levels of theological urgency. While it may not always be perfectly clear which category a doctrine falls into, this structure can, at the very least, guide us toward the issues that are of greatest importance. Debate that is most helpful will be debate that takes into consideration the relative importance of the particular issue.

First-level issues are those that are most central and essential to the Christian faith. This includes the doctrines of the Trinity, atonement, the deity and humanity of Jesus Christ, justification by faith alone, and the authority of Scripture. Those who deny any of these doctrines are denying truths that are absolutely and fundamentally

<hr>

[9]Albert Mohler, "A Call for Theological Triage and Christian Maturity" (http://www.crosswalk.com/news/weblogs/mohler/?adate=7/12/2005).

essential to the Christian faith. Denial of these key doctrines necessarily represents the abandonment of biblical Christianity.

Second-level issues are doctrines that believers may disagree on but which still represent important issues and will form significant boundaries between Christians. These are often the doctrines that have defined or divided denominations. Examples might include the mode and meaning of baptism or the continuing miraculous gifts of the Holy Spirit. While Christians from either camp will affirm that those on the other side of the disagreement are brothers or sisters in Christ and will share fellowship with them on some level, these people will always experience a level of disagreement that will likely preclude greater unity.

Third-level issues are those over which Christians may disagree even while maintaining close fellowship and remaining in the same local church. These may include doctrines such as the end times or whether Christians may consume alcohol in moderation.

A caution is in order. Mohler writes, "A structure of theological triage does not imply that Christians may take any biblical truth with less than full seriousness. We are charged to embrace and to teach the comprehensive truthfulness of the Christian faith as revealed in the Holy Scriptures. There are no insignificant doctrines revealed in the Bible, but there is an essential foundation of truth that undergirds the entire system of biblical truth." As men and women of discernment, we should focus our efforts on matters that are of the greatest consequence. Our efforts in discernment are most important when the issues at stake are issues that sit at the very heart of the Christian faith. We must ensure that we do not become distracted by smaller issues when foundational matters are being disputed and are under attack.

AREAS OF DISCERNMENT

Question 3 of the Westminster Shorter Catechism asks, "What do the Scriptures principally teach?" The answer is simple: "The Scriptures principally teach what man is to believe concerning God, and what duty God requires of man." These are the two great and related thrusts of Scripture: teaching truth and then explaining how this truth applies to us. The Bible teaches the faith and the requirement of this faith. We must not overlook the order here. Beliefs come before duty. We saw in a previous chapter that the book of Proverbs has a similar set of priorities, placing character before conduct, for what we believe will necessarily impact how we act. The Shorter Catechism is structured around these two categories; questions 4 to 38 speak of what the Bible teaches about God, and questions 39 to107 speak of man's duty of obedience to God. Reflecting on this, G. I. Williamson writes, "Let us emphasize the fact that the Catechism firmly rejects the choice between Christianity as a doctrine and Christianity as a life. True Christianity is never one without the other. It is always both together: like the good tree and the good fruit."[10]

Just as the two great themes of Scripture are teaching what we are to believe concerning God and the duty associated with such knowledge and such faith, the purpose of testing doctrine is to reveal to us two great categories of understanding: the truth of God and the will of God. Like the Catechism, spiritual discernment also rejects the choice between Christianity as a doctrine and Christianity as a life. Discernment depends on knowing that Christianity is both belief and action. It is action based on belief.

In our definition of discernment we saw that discernment has both a theological and a moral dimension, and we saw this in the portion of the definition that spoke of "truth from error and right from wrong." The first category where we need to exercise discernment is that of truth and error in relation to what we believe about God. The second category is that of right and wrong in relation to how we act. The first category relates to truth and discernment and the second to God's will and discernment. These are the two broad categories in which we need to exercise spiritual discernment. The next two chapters will discuss these topics in greater detail. We will see that discernment is the practice that allows us first to know the truth of God and then to know and do the will of God.

---

[10]G. I. Williamson, *The Shorter Catechism*, Vol. 1, Questions 1–38 (Phillipsburg, NJ: Presbyterian and Reformed, 1970), 13

KEY THOUGHT

Spiritual discernment requires that we carefully test and prove everything associated with Christian life and doctrine. Though all that God teaches about himself is important, we must focus our efforts in discernment on the doctrines that are most foundational to the Christian faith. The two areas where we must practice spiritual discernment are the same as the two general themes of Scripture: what we must believe about God and how God calls us to live on the basis of those beliefs or, said otherwise, the truth of God and the will of God.

chapter five

TRUTH and DISCERNMENT

*Walk as children of light
(for the fruit of light is found in all that is good and right and true),
and try to discern what is pleasing to the Lord.*

EPHESIANS 5:8B–10

ON JUNE 2, 2006, Secret Service agents made an unexpected visit to the offices of the Great News Network, a Christian organization that trains evangelists. The agents approached Tim Crawford, a staff member, and asked if he was the man responsible for printing "million dollar bills." Crawford directed the agents to his boss, Darrel Rundus, the man who founded the organization. Among the products distributed by the Great News Network is a tract produced by the Living Waters Ministry of Ray Comfort. Designed to look like an imaginary million-dollar bill and featuring a portrait of the great preacher Charles Spurgeon, the tracts are clearly marked "this bill is not legal tender." The back contains an evangelistic message designed to provide a brief explanation of the gospel. Agents told Rundus that a woman in North Carolina had attempted to deposit one of the bills in her bank account. The Secret Service had become involved and was intent on tracking down the source of these phony bank notes. Though the agents eventually left without pressing charges, they confiscated over eight thousand of these tracts.

Rundus, clearly bemused by the situation, made an astute observation: it is impossible to counterfeit something that is not real. Because there is no genuine million-dollar bill, agents cannot rationally accuse anyone of counterfeiting one. "Show me the law we're breaking," he told WorldNetDaily. "How can you counterfeit bills that do not exist?"[1] Rundus raised an interesting point, one that shows the ridiculous nature of this situation. For an object to be counterfeit, it must model itself on something that actually exists. Without some basis in reality it is mere fiction.

Five years earlier, in 2001, police in Windsor, Ontario, shut down a counterfeiting operation that had produced a large quantity of phony hundred-dollar bills. Before the authorities were able to put an end to this operation a limited number of these bills had entered circulation. Because of its proximity to the United States, the city of Windsor is the location of a large number of national head offices for Canadian corporations. Word of the counterfeit currency traveled quickly from national offices in Windsor to regional ones across the country. A senior analyst within the Bank of Canada said, "This certainly led to the perception that the problem was more widespread than it actually was." From these offices spread word of the counterfeit money, and soon businesses across the nation were refusing to accept any hundred-dollar bills, fearful that they might accept a phony bill. Even today many Canadian businesses refuse all hundred-dollar bills.

Does either one of these stories describe a crime? Or is it possible that *both* stories do?

The Bank of Canada produces a hundred-dollar bill. Thus, when counterfeiters printed a reproduction of it and exchanged that fraudulent bill for goods, they were committing a serious crime. In the introduction to this book we saw just how serious a crime counterfeiting can be! It is a crime that can disrupt and even destroy a nation's economy. The men responsible were justly convicted and

[1]Joseph Farah, "Feds Seize Millions—In Gospel Tracts" (http://www.worldnetdaily.com/news/article.asp?ARTICLE_ID=50495).

were sentenced to time in prison. On the other hand, the United States has no million-dollar bill, and thus the tract produced by Living Waters Ministry was mere fiction. It did not represent something that actually exists. The Windsor hundred-dollar bills were counterfeit, but the Living Waters tracts were not. The difference between these two stories is clear: for something to be counterfeit it must attempt to represent something that is genuine.

The practice of spiritual discernment is founded on a belief in the existence of both error and truth. This is not the subjective truth of a postmodern society but a full-blown, objective truth—the "true truth" of Christianity. When a person counterfeits Christian doctrine, he is not printing a million-dollar bill, creating a fictitious representation of something that could be. Rather, he is distorting what is really, truly, objectively true and is committing a serious crime against God. In this chapter we will examine the existence of truth and show that discernment can only exist where truth is affirmed. Discernment depends on an understanding that objective truth and error both exist and are in constant opposition to one another. The practice of discernment involves judging between what is true and what is false.

TRUE TRUTH

Over three decades ago Francis Schaeffer coined the delightfully ambiguous phrase "true truth." Here is how he described this term in his book *Escape from Reason*:

> It is an important principle to remember, in the contemporary interest in communication and in language study, that the biblical presentation is that though we do not have exhaustive truth, we have from the Bible what I term "true truth." In this way we know true truth about God, true truth about man, and something truly about nature. Thus on the basis of the Scriptures, while we do not have exhaustive knowledge, we have true and unified knowledge.[2]

We do not know everything there is to know, but what God

<hr>

[2]Francis Schaeffer, *Trilogy* (Wheaton, IL: Crossway Books, 1990), 218.

teaches us through creation and through the Bible is indeed both true and trustworthy. "People today live in a generation that no longer believes in the hope of truth as truth. That is why I use the term 'true truth' in my books to emphasize real truth. This is not just tautology. It is an admission that the word *truth* now means something that [before the advent of the philosophers Rousseau, Kant, Hegel, and Kierkegaard] would not have been considered truth at all. So I coined the expression 'true truth' to make the point, but it is hard to make it sharp enough for people to understand how large the problem is."[3] In an address at the University of Notre Dame in April of 1981 Schaeffer said, "Christianity is not a series of truths in the plural, but rather truth spelled with a capital 'T.' Truth about total reality, not just about religious things. Biblical Christianity is Truth concerning total reality—and the intellectual holding of that total Truth and then living in the light of that Truth."[4]

And what is truth? "Here's a simple definition drawn from what the Bible teaches: *Truth is that which is consistent with the mind, will, character, glory, and being of God.* Even more to the point: *truth is the self-expression of God.* That is the biblical meaning of truth. . . . Truth is *theological.*"[5] Truth is what God thinks; it is what God does; it is what God is; it is what God has revealed of himself in the Bible. Truth is found in its fullest form in God, for he is truth; he is the very source and origin of all truth.

It is important to realize, though, that while God is truth, truth does not equal God. Were we to equate truth with God, we would make truth something we could worship and adore. Truth is not a standard that God needs to live up to in order to be true to himself. Rather, he is the source of truth and all that is true flows from him.

Many who profess to believe in Christ affirm Christianity as a collection of truths, and even very important, life-altering truths, but not as Truth; not as a worldview that encompasses all of life. To be people of discernment, we must acknowledge the existence of

---

[3]Ibid., 310–11 (emphasis added).
[4]As quoted in Nancy Pearcey, *Total Truth: Liberating Christianity from Its Cultural Captivity* (Wheaton, IL: Crossway Books, 2005), 15.
[5]John MacArthur, *The Truth War* (Nashville: Thomas Nelson, 2007), 2.

both truth and error. And, just as there will always be counterfeit currency, where there is truth, there will be counterfeits of the truth. Our task as people of discernment is to separate what is truth from what is error. It is to ensure that we think of God and believe in God in ways that are consistent with how he has revealed himself to us in the Bible. Our confidence is not in ourselves, but that God has made his truth clear to us. We have confidence that God is capable of communicating to us in a way that we will be able to understand.

THE SOURCE OF TRUTH

God is the source of truth, for he *is* truth. We know of truth and we know of God through the Bible. The Bible was given to us to guide us to Jesus Christ, and the Bible is a book that speaks primarily of his work. We know the Bible is true because it is the revelation of God, who is true and who is unable to lie. There can be no imperfection in the Bible because there is no imperfection in God.

The fullest expression of truth is in the person of Jesus Christ. All that Jesus did, said, and thought was true. Truth is both fixed and constant. It is not changing or something to be created. Good and evil are realities that are both extrinsic to us. The forces of good and evil are not determined by our choices or preferences. In opposition to the dominant mindset of our day, something is not evil simply because it is not in accord with what we feel or desire, and neither is something else good because we like it or enjoy it. Rather, things are objectively good or evil regardless of how or what we may feel about them. This is why we must determine whether something is good or evil, right or wrong, based on the objective, unmoving standard of the Bible rather than on our subjective, constantly-shifting feelings and preferences.

As sinful human beings we are prone to give undue authority to our feelings and to interpret truth on the basis of what we feel. The biblical paradigm is exactly the opposite and commands us to interpret our feelings on the basis of truth. C. J. Mahaney warns about this, saying, "The humble are those whose first response to objective truth from God's Word is not to ask, 'How do I feel?' but to say, 'I'm not going to let my faith be determined and directed by the subjective and the experiential. Instead I confess openly before God that I will believe the objective truth of His Word, regardless of how I feel."[6]

John Piper writes, "The reason there is such a thing as objective good outside ourselves is that there is God outside ourselves. And most concretely and specifically, God has made himself known objectively and historically in Jesus Christ in Scripture."[7] We are given the opportunity to prove our understanding of truth and error as we seek to do God's will, a topic that will be the subject of our next chapter. A discerning Christian will be one who returns constantly to the Word of God, the source of all truth.

THINKING RIGHTLY ABOUT GOD

To be Christians who have what is truly a Christian worldview, it is critical that we think rightly about God. A.W. Tozer began *The Knowledge of the Holy,* his most highly acclaimed book, with these words: "What comes into our minds when we think about God is the most important thing about us." No person or religion has ever been greater than its idea of God, and worship is seen as being true or false on the basis of its high or low thoughts of God. Tozer goes on to say:

> For this reason the gravest question before the Church is always God Himself, and the most portentous fact about any man is not what he at any given time may say or do, but what he in his deep heart conceives God to be like. . . . Were we able to extract from any man a complete answer to the question, "What comes into your mind when you think about God?" we might predict with certainty the spiritual future of that man. Without doubt, the mightiest thought the mind can entertain is the thought of God, and the weightiest word in any language is its word for God.[8]

---

[6]C. J. Mahaney, *Living the Cross Centered Life: Keeping the Gospel the Main Thing* (Sisters, OR: Multnomah, 2006), 35.
[7]John Piper, "Abhor What Is Evil; Hold Fast to What Is Good" (http://www.desiringgod.org/ResourceLibrary/Sermons/ByDate/2004/191_Abhor_What_Is_Evil_Hold_Fast_to_What_Is_Good/).
[8]A. W. Tozer, *The Knowledge of the Holy* (New York: HerperOne, 1978), 1–2.

We must think rightly about God, because what we believe necessarily impacts what we do. What we do is premised on what we believe. Thus the closer our thoughts are to the reality of who God is and what he is like, the more our lives will be a reflection of him. Tozer says that any error in doctrine or any failure to properly apply the theology of the Bible to our lives can be traced to wrong thoughts about God.[9] Read the Bible and study the history of the church and you'll soon see just how right he is—how our thoughts of God shape our service for him. When we think wrong thoughts about God we soon serve him in wrong ways as well. We must get our theology right!

Tozer wrote this book, which went on to become a Christian classic, to encourage believers to elevate their concept of God until it is worthy of him and until it is an accurate reflection of him. There is nothing Christians could do that would prove to be of greater value than this.

And so the first area in which we must exercise discernment is our thoughts of God. Our theology must accurately reflect God as he has chosen to reveal himself. We must dedicate ourselves to the pursuit of knowing and understanding God by separating what is true about God from what is false. Ignore this discipline, J. I. Packer warns, and "you sentence yourself to stumble and blunder through life blindfold, as it were, with no sense of direction and no understanding of what surrounds you. This way you can waste your life and lose your soul."[10]

If we are going to know God by knowing what is true about him, we must be people who have their doctrine right. We must be people who know what we believe and believe it with conviction. There are some within the church who believe that "doctrine divides" and yet Christ taught otherwise. In his High Priestly Prayer, he said,

> "Sanctify them in the truth; your word is truth. As you sent me into the world, so I have sent them into the world. And for their sake I consecrate myself, that they also may be sanctified in truth.

---

[9]Ibid., 4.
[10]J. I. Packer, *Knowing God* (London: Hodder & Stoughton, 1973), 17.

> "I do not ask for these only, but also for those who will
> believe in me through their word, that they may all be one, just
> as you, Father, are in me, and I in you, that they also may be in
> us, so that the world may believe that you have sent me." (John
> 17:17–21)

Jesus asked God for unity within the church ("that they may
all be one") on the basis of truth. Truth is not meant to divide but
to unify. Discernment will allow us to understand what is true and
thus bring unity to the church and glory to God. Sound doctrine,
doctrine that is consistent with the Bible, is absolutely foundational
to healthy Christians. We cannot and must not deemphasize this.

WORLDLINESS

Spiritual discernment is our frontline defense against worldliness,
the very opposite of thinking rightly about God.

> Worldliness is departing from God. It is a man-centered way of
> thinking; it proposes objectives which demand no radical breach
> with man's fallen nature; it judges the importance of things by
> the present and material results; it weighs success by numbers;
> it covets human esteem and wants no unpopularity; it knows no
> truth for which it is worth suffering; it declines to be a "fool for
> Christ's sake." Worldliness is the mindset of the unregenerate. It
> adopts idols and is at war with God.[11]

Where thinking rightly about God will lead us always to Jesus
Christ, and always to the cross, worldliness, a lack of discernment,
will lead us to ourselves. It will judge the validity of a teaching not
by the objective and unchanging standards of what Scripture says
to be true but by what is seen and understood in the here and now.
"Never criticize what God is blessing" or "If it works, God must
be behind it" are statements that reflect a pragmatic worldview
that looks to results rather than Scripture as the arbiter of truth
and error. When our minds are so tainted by sin, we will allow all
manner of gross error into our lives and into the church simply

---

[11]Iain Murray, *Evangelicalism Divided: A Record of Crucial Change in the Years 1950 to 2000*
(Edinburgh: Banner of Truth, 2000), 255.

because, through our limited understanding, we feel the end justifies the means.

Men and women of discernment will separate truth and error not on the basis of what seems to work but on the basis of the unchanging truth of the Bible. They will not be fooled or led astray by pragmatism but will return always to the Scripture.

THE TEST OF TRUTH

My mother recently mentioned to me a phenomenon she has begun to notice around the Christmas season. She was recently at one of America's largest home-and-garden centers choosing a Christmas tree, and she was surprised to hear Christmas carols playing over the speakers. These were not carols of the "Rudolph the Red-Nosed Reindeer" variety but traditional carols speaking of the person and work of Jesus Christ. But as she listened to these songs, she noticed something strange: whenever the original lyrics to the carols mentioned the name of Jesus, his name had been replaced by a pronoun. In the words to Charles Wesley's "Hark! The Herald Angels Sing," she heard, "with the angelic host proclaim / 'He is born in Bethlehem.'" The name of Jesus had been removed.

And yet it is this name, the name of Jesus, which is the theme of Christmas and, indeed, the theme of all of Scripture. The entire Bible points to the person and work of Jesus Christ. The Old Testament, in all its covenants, sacrifices, and prophecies, points forward to him, and the New Testament, in all its theology and history, points back to him. It is little wonder, then, that those who are opposed to God despise the name of Jesus.

How is it that we know we are worshiping God in truth? How do we know that we are worshiping him in a way that is consistent with what he has revealed of himself in the Bible? J. I. Packer provides the following test of truth:

> The test is this. The God of the Bible has spoken in his Son. The light of the knowledge of his glory is given us in the face of Jesus Christ. Do I look habitually to the person and work of the Lord Jesus Christ as showing me the final truth about the nature and

grace of God? Do I see all the purposes of God as centring upon him?

If I have been enabled to see this, and in mind and heart to go to Calvary and lay hold of the Calvary solution, then I can know that I truly worship the true God, and that he is my God, and that I am even now enjoying eternal life, according to our Lord's own definition, "Now this is eternal life: that they may know you the only true God, and Jesus Christ, whom you have sent" (John 17:3).[12]

When Jesus Christ is exalted, when his name is honored, then we know we are seeking the true God. Other faiths lead in opposite directions: Islam teaches that Jesus is but a prophet and not uniquely the Son of God; the Jehovah's Witnesses teach that Jesus is a god, but a lesser god than the Father; the New Age teaches that Jesus was a great man, but that he was no more divine than you or I. Every other faith leads us away from the beauty and uniqueness of Jesus Christ. When Jesus is magnified, we know that we are pursuing what is true. We are being led by the Spirit to a greater understanding of God and the glory and majesty of his Son.

In his letter to the church at Philippi, Paul writes, "It is my prayer that your love may abound more and more, with knowledge and all discernment, so that you may approve what is excellent" (Phil. 1:9–10). Testing our doctrine to ensure that it points always to Jesus Christ will show us what is excellent in God's eyes. The things that are excellent are "all the truths, attitudes, thoughts, words, and deeds that are expressions of God's will for the believer. They are the elements of sanctified, holy thinking and living."[13] What is excellent is all that is good and right and true. To be those who honor Christ in the way we live our lives, we must discern what is pleasing to him. We must separate what is true from what is false and live in the light of that truth.

THE RELATIONSHIP OF TRUTH TO ERROR

In 1910 the Carnegie Foundation released a report entitled *Medical Education in the United States and Canada*. Researched and writ-

---

[12]J. I. Packer, *Knowing God*, 55.
[13]John MacArthur, *Philippians* (Chicago: Moody, 2000), 47.

ten by an educator named Abraham Flexner, this report triggered widespread reform in the field of medical education. Flexner found that many medical schools were motivated more by profit than by a desire to properly educate doctors. These schools often accredited doctors after only two years of study. Meanwhile, oversight from state and national governments ranged between sporadic and nonexistent. Flexner addressed these shortcomings with sweeping recommendations that would have a deep and lasting impact that is still felt today. His recommendations forced changes in health care across North America that has led health care on this continent to become among the best in the world.

One of Flexner's most important recommendations dealt with the proper order of classes in medical school. There were to be four years of intensive training, the first two dealing with basic science and the following two with clinical training. These first two years were broken into two fundamental science blocks, "the first year being devoted to learning normal human anatomy and physiology and the second year focusing on abnormal physiology and the disruptions of disease."[14] Even today, most medical schools follow this established pattern, focusing first on what is normal and good and only later teaching what is irregular—the result of disease and abnormality.

This aspect of Flexner's report points to something that is also true about truth. We can best know what is wrong by first knowing what is right. Experts on counterfeit currency know this as well. They train others first to know the traits of genuine currency because such knowledge will make apparent what is fraudulent. Christians need to dedicate themselves to learning and knowing truth so that what is evil and abnormal will appear obvious. For this reason the apostle writes, "Finally, brothers, whatever is true, whatever is honorable, whatever is just, whatever is pure, whatever is lovely, whatever is commendable, if there is any excellence, if there is anything worthy of praise, think about these things" (Phil. 4:8). He encourages us to think first and foremost about what is right and true and pure and lovely. In Romans 16:19b he says this

---

[14]Pauline Chen, *Final Exam* (New York: Alfred Knopf, 2007), 135.

as well, exhorting the Roman church "to be wise as to what is good and innocent as to what is evil." Never does the Bible tell us to dwell primarily or repeatedly upon what is false.

The relationship of truth to error is such that we can best know error by knowing truth. The opposite is not true. People who invest undue effort in concentrating upon what is false will not necessarily be able to identify what is true. By dwelling upon the beautiful truths of Scripture we will subsequently learn discernment. A discerning person will know that he must focus his heart upon what is true and pure and lovely, having confidence that in doing this God will bless him with the ability to expose darkness.

THE SUBTLETY OF ERROR

I have had people approach me asking me to evaluate books for them, books that are filled with the most pernicious lies, books filled with statements absolutely antithetical to Christianity. I have had people hand me books by leading New Age authors and ask, "What do you think of this book?" Such people, though they may be genuine Christians, exhibit a shocking inability to discern truth from error. In fact, it seems that many of these people hardly believe that error is a force that should concern them. As often as not they seem to be interested in knowing whether a book is good as measured by some subjective standard of excitement or interest rather than whether the book is true and good by the objective standard of God's Word.

We cannot affirm the existence of truth without also affirming the existence of error. Where one exists, so will the other. Error will pervert our thoughts of God, filling our minds with ideas of God that are unworthy of him and not in accordance with what the Bible teaches about him. And when our thoughts of God are wrong, our actions will soon also be wrong. Just as J. I. Packer's test of truth will show if we are pursuing truth, it can show if we are pursuing error. When our eyes are taken off the cross, when the gospel becomes secondary, when we are made the center of our faith, we know that we are pursuing what is wrong.

Error is not always obvious and so we need to be aware of the subtlety of error. This was clearly a problem in the early church. "For certain people have crept in unnoticed who long ago were designated for this condemnation, ungodly people, who pervert the grace of our God into sensuality and deny our only Master and Lord, Jesus Christ" (Jude 4). By increasing our discernment and by practicing discernment we can grow in our knowledge of the truth so that which is error becomes increasingly obvious. Even subtle error will appear with clarity. R. C. H. Lenski writes, "The worst forms of wickedness consist of perversions of the truth, of spiritual lies, although today many look upon these forms with indifference and regard them rather harmless"[15]

It is easy to be duped into thinking that just a little error is harmless and will not matter. And yet Scripture teaches otherwise. Pastor and author Joshua Harris speaks of "half a poison pill" to describe the mindset of many Christians in which they think repeated exposure to just a little bit of evil will not harm them. These Christians seem to think they have a sin threshold beyond which they dare not go. Yet these people may as well ask just how much of a poison pill they need to swallow before it kills them. "The greatest danger of the popular media is not a one-time exposure to a particular instance of sin (as serious as that can be). It's how long-term exposure to worldliness—little chunks of poison pill, day after day, week after week—can deaden our hearts to the ugliness of sin."[16] Repeated exposure to error can lead us to unwittingly swallow a lethal dose. Error may be subtle but it is always deadly.

BLACK, WHITE, AND GRAY

On March 7, 1990, Patty Hensel gave birth to twin girls in a hospital in Carver County, Minnesota. As the result of a rare abnormality, Abby and Brittany were born as dicephalic conjoined twins, meaning that they have two heads but only one body. Each of the girls controls one side of the conjoined body but has no sensation in the

---

[15]R. C. H. Lenski, *The Interpretation of St. Paul's Epistles to the Colossians, to the Thessalonians, to Timothy, to Titus and to Philemon* (Minneapolis: Augsburg, 1961), 363.
[16]Joshua Harris, "Like to Watch" (http://www.boundless.org/2005/articles/a0001258.cfm).

other side. Each controls one of the two arms and one of the two legs. Internally they have two hearts, two sets of lungs, two stomachs, and two large intestines. Yet they share a circulatory system, a small intestine and bowel, and their reproductive organs. In some ways they are two people but in other ways they are one.

These girls redefine individuality. At school they each write their own English tests and are graded individually, yet in math they work together and receive a single grade. On their sixteenth birthday they took their driver's tests and had to take the test twice, even though driving is a collaborative effort in which they share the steering responsibilities while one works the brakes and the gas and the other works the turn signals. They passed both tests and each of the two girls received her own license. When they use the instant messaging program on their computer, they both type (one controlling the left hand and the other the right) and tend to use the pronoun *I* when they express a view they share (rather than *we*). Again, in some ways they seem to be two people and in other ways they seem to be one. Whenever they face a new situation in life, they have to determine whether they will be treated as one person or two.

The girls raise a host of questions. If they are caught speeding which one of them will get the speeding ticket? When they go to college will they have to pay tuition for one or for two? When they fly, do they need to purchase two tickets or only one? Some problems cut much deeper. What if the girls want to marry? The girls have indicated that they wish to be mothers someday. They are normal in more ways than not, and like most girls they want to experience motherhood. It seems that, physically, they will be able to bear children. They also seem to want to experience the joys of romance and marriage. But how can they do this when they are both individuals and conjoined? Should the two of them marry a single man? Or should they marry individually? If they do give birth to a baby, whose baby will it be?

As we have already seen, discernment is a discipline that depends upon making binary distinctions. It involves separating good from bad, truth from error, right from wrong, better from best. In other words, it involves separating black from white and seems to leave little room for gray. When we practice discernment, we are applying the truths of the Bible to our lives and are trusting the Word of God to give clarity so that we might see things as God sees them.

Yet sometimes it seems that clarity is impossible. How can we have absolute clarity about situations like the one posed by Abby and Brittany Hensel? How can we fully and finally determine how romance, marriage, sex, and childbearing can work in this type of a situation? There are many biblical principles that can guide us, but it seems that none of them are extensive enough or complete enough to govern this. There are many other situations in life that seem more gray than black or white. How does discernment function in such gray times? Here are a few principles that can guide us as we wrestle with the gray issues:

Rarity

It is important to affirm that truly gray situations are rare. Most often the gray situations are gray only because we have not done enough work to clarify them or because our own sinful desires have interfered and have interposed themselves between black and white.

The Fall

We also need to affirm that "grayness" is a result of the fall. Were we perfect beings we would not have to wrestle with the host of issues that fall somewhere between black and white. It is only our sin that forces us to have to deal with issues that would otherwise be clear. There is no reason to think that issues like this will trouble us when we are in heaven.

Clarity

When wrestling with issues that appear gray, it is important to begin with what the Bible makes clear. Far too often we begin with what is obscure and work backwards to what is clear so that the exception disproves the rule. As Christians we must begin with what God has made clear in his Word. When looking at the Hensel girls we would not want to allow their unique situation to change our minds about what the Bible says plainly: that God demands and expects that marriage is the union of one man to one woman and that any deviations from this pattern make a mockery of the whole institution of marriage. We need to begin with the Bible and allow it to establish the standard. We can then interpret deviations or exceptions on the basis of this unmoving standard.

Humility

Gray situations provide us an opportunity to express humility. When we come to the end of our abilities and realize that we simply are unable to see with the clarity of God, we can take the opportunity to see again that we are mere creatures. We lack the perspective and the wisdom of the Creator, and this should help us express our humility before him.

Dependence

Gray situations also give us the opportunity to express dependence on this Creator. There are times when even our best efforts fall short. There are times when even our best attempts at extrapolating the Bible's wisdom leave us scratching our heads. This gives us opportunity to express our dependence on the Spirit and to acknowledge that any ability in spiritual discernment is a gift from above.

Conscience

These gray situations show the need for a developed, biblically-informed conscience. Sometimes, when we simply cannot arrive at a firm and satisfying conclusion, we need to rely on something that goes just a little bit deeper than pure reason. It seems that God has given us a conscience for this reason. While conscience must be subservient to Scripture and informed by it, it nevertheless plays an important role in the life of the Christian and should often be heeded, especially when the issues are less than perfectly clear to us.

It is frustrating to me that these gray situations exist. Yet it seems that they can be healthy. Not only can they stimulate a lot of thought, a lot of discussion, and a lot of searching of the Scriptures, but they also teach us about the need for dependence upon the Lord and the need for humility. It is crucial that we maintain our emphasis on discernment even when the issues are not as clear as we might like.

Spiritual discernment equips us to believe in God in a way that is consistent with his revelation of himself. It equips us to know him rightly so that we might serve him rightly. It allows us to examine any doctrine or any teaching and to separate what is truth from what is error. We use the Word of God, the Bible, to guide us in this process. The discerning Christian will be the one who compares everything to Scripture, always seeking to know what is true about God.

When we are people that honor God with how we think of him and how we know him, we are people that are prepared and equipped to know and do the will of God. We have prepared our character so God can now address conduct. We have addressed truth so we can now live in light of that truth. And so in our next chapter we will discuss discernment in the context of understanding and obeying God's will for our lives.

KEY THOUGHT

To be people that honor God with our actions, we must first be people who honor God in what we think of him and what we believe to be true about him. Only when we think rightly about God will we live in a way that is consistent with his will for our lives. Spiritual discernment will equip us to know God as he has revealed himself and thus allow us to avoid having worldly hearts and minds.

the WILL and DISCERNMENT

*Do not be conformed to this world, but be transformed by the
renewal of your mind, that by testing you may discern what is the will
of God, what is good and acceptable and perfect.*

ROMANS 12:2

WE SAW IN CHAPTER THREE that many Christians, and perhaps even most Christians, draw an immediate connection between
discernment and the will of God. In the past two chapters I have
attempted to show that discernment is concerned primarily with
the truth of God. Having seen this and having understood that the
task of the Christian is to strive to seek out and obey the truth of
God, we are now prepared to understand how discernment relates
to God's will. We will see that the will of God is founded upon and
inseparable from what is true about God.

Theologians speak of God's will in two ways, though as tends
to happen with theologians, they use a variety of terms to describe
these two ways. The traditional terms are God's decretive will and
God's preceptive will—hardly words we encounter on a daily basis.
These are also known as God's will of decree and God's will of command or, perhaps most simply, God's secret will and his revealed

will. Of course the terms matters far less than the definition and the application, so we will turn to this now.

It is my belief and my experience that much of the confusion in the church about what Christians are to believe and how they are to act stems from a poor understanding of the will of God. Christians absorb many words and phrases and ways of speaking without fully understanding what they mean. When people speak of desiring to know God's will, they may intend to speak of one aspect of his will while unknowingly speaking of another. Hence it is critical that we distinguish between them. R.C. Sproul writes the following:

> The practical question of how we know the will of God for our lives cannot be solved with any degree of accuracy unless we have some prior understanding of the will of God in general. Without the distinctions we have made, our pursuit of the will of God can plunge us into hopeless confusion and consternation. When we seek the will of God, we must first ask ourselves which will we are seeking to discover.[1]

Lest we plunge into hopeless confusion, let's differentiate between these two aspects of God's will.

GOD'S WILL OF DECREE

God's will of decree is his secret will. It is the will that has existed fully and finally since before the creation of the earth. It is the will through which God has decreed all that will happen. The Westminster Shorter Catechism says, "The decrees of God are, his eternal purpose, according to the counsel of his will, whereby, for his own glory, he hath foreordained whatsoever comes to pass." In eternity past God decreed all that will happen, and nothing and no one can change or interrupt this will. It is the will spoken of by the prophet Isaiah who writes:

> "I am God, and there is no other;
>   I am God, and there is none like me,
>   declaring the end from the beginning

---

[1]R. C. Sproul, *Can I Know God's Will?* (Orlando, FL: Ligonier, 1999), 33–34.

> and from ancient times things not yet done,
> saying, 'My counsel shall stand,
>   and I will accomplish all my purpose,'
>   calling a bird of prey from the east,
>   the man of my counsel from a far country.
> I have spoken, and I will bring it to pass;
>   I have purposed, and I will do it." (Isa. 46:9–11)

In this passage God reveals his absolute sovereignty over all of Creation. He alone rules all things through all times. He rules the actions of the birds and the choices of human beings.

Whatever he has purposed, whatever he has decided upon, will come to pass. There is none who can thwart or interrupt this will and nothing can happen outside of it.

As difficult as it is to believe, God's secret will extends even to things that are evil, though God himself does no wrong ("his work is perfect, for all his ways are justice. A God of faithfulness and without iniquity, just and upright is he" [Deut. 32:4].) He does decree that evil will take place. After all, the Bible tells us that the single most horrible, sinful act in human history, the crucifixion of Jesus Christ, was predestined to take place. In Acts 4, after Jesus' resurrection, the disciples prayed together, saying to God, "In this city there were gathered together against your holy servant Jesus, whom you anointed, both Herod and Pontius Pilate, along with the Gentiles and the peoples of Israel, to do whatever your hand and your plan had predestined to take place" (Acts 4:27–28). God's hand and plan had predestined that his precious Son would be brutally slaughtered.

God's secret will is hidden to us. God chooses not to reveal it to us and it does not figure into our decision making because it is, by definition, secret. So when we speak of discerning God's will, we do not speak of this, his secret will. This will, predestined before time began, is set in stone and *will* be accomplished. There is nothing we can do to change it or to alter it. God reveals it as he wills, and we are unable to know it beyond his ways of revealing it. "The secret things belong to the LORD our God, but the things that are revealed belong to us and to our children forever, that we may do all the words of this law" (Deut. 29:29). R. C. Sproul warns of the foolishness of speculating about the hidden will of the Lord:

> If our quest is to penetrate the hidden aspects of his will, then we have embarked on a fool's errand. We are trying the impossible and chasing the untouchable. Such a quest is not only an act of foolishness but an act of presumption. There is a very real sense in which the secret will of the secret counsel of God is none of our business and is off limits to our speculative investigations.
>
> Untold evils have been perpetrated upon the church and upon God's people by unscrupulous theologians who have sought to correct or to supplant the clear and plain teaching of sacred Scripture by doctrines and theories based on speculation alone. The business of searching out the mind of God where God has remained silent is dangerous business indeed. Luther put it this way: "We must keep in view His Word and leave alone His inscrutable will; for it is by His Word and not by His inscrutable will that we must be guided." [2]

Knowing that God's secret will is off-limits to us, we turn now to the things that are revealed.

GOD'S WILL OF COMMAND

While God's will of decree is his secret will, his will of command is his revealed will that directs how we are to live. His revealed will is all those things he tells us to do in the Bible and the things he has written upon our conscience. It is all those things he expects us to do to bring honor to him. First Thessalonians 4:3 provides a succinct summary of God's will: "For this is the will of God, your sanctification." Through the commands given us in Scripture, God tells us how we may be sanctified and how we may be ever-more conformed into the image of his Son. It is God's will for each of us that we grow in holiness, that we grow in our knowledge and love of God, and that we let the love of God shine through us.

The Bible says a great deal about this will. There are some passages that speak of God's will in very specific matters and others

---

[2]Ibid.

that are more general and provide a framework. Here are three of these general principles:

1) Be Filled with the Holy Spirit

It is God's will that we be filled with the Holy Spirit. "Therefore do not be foolish, but understand what the will of the Lord is. And do not get drunk with wine, for that is debauchery, but be filled with the Spirit" (Eph. 5:17–18).

2) Be Sanctified

It is God's will that we be sanctified and that we continue to grow more and more into the image of Jesus Christ. "For this is the will of God, your sanctification" (1 Thess. 4:3a).

3) Be Thankful

We are to be thankful at all times and in all situations. "Give thanks in all circumstances; for this is the will of God in Christ Jesus for you" (1 Thess. 5:18).

These three commands intersect with all areas of life and display God's revealed will for us. It is this will that the apostle Paul discusses in Romans 12, where he clearly connects discernment and God's will. "Do not be conformed to this world," Paul writes, "but be transformed by the renewal of your mind, that by testing you may discern what is the will of God, what is good and acceptable and perfect" (v. 2). Here the Bible tells us that by testing we will be able to discern the will of God. In the Greek the words *testing* and *discern* are one, a word which is often translated as "prove" or "try." It means "to test, examine, prove, scrutinize (to see whether a thing is genuine or not) . . . to recognize as genuine after examination, to approve, deem worthy."[3] This will of command does not include God's decree but his will as to what we should do in order to please him and in order to live in such a way that we bring honor to his name. This will was given in days past through the priests,

---

[3] James Strong, *The Exhaustive Concordance of the Bible: Showing Every Word of the Text of the Common English Version of the Canonical Books, and Every Occurrence of Each Word in Regular Order*, electronic ed. (Ontario: Woodside Bible Fellowship, 1996).

through the mysterious Urim and Thummin, and through judges and prophets. Today it is given to us in its full and final measure in the Bible, the Word of God.

Ephesians 5 is a passage that in many ways parallels Romans 12. This passage also draws a line between discovering truth and discerning God's will. "Walk as children of light (for the fruit of light is found in all that is good and right and true), and try to discern what is pleasing to the Lord" (Eph. 5:8b–10). By searching for what is good and right and true, we discover God's will. A desire to seek and practice truth is a distinguishing characteristic of those who believe. Sinclair Ferguson points out that "despite the ESV translation, there is no verb *try to* but a present participle of the verb to *discern*. So Paul is saying *Walk as children of the light . . .* discerning what is pleasing to the Lord."[4]

If we are to discover the will of God, we first need to discern what is pleasing to him. We do this by imitating Christ who modeled perfect discernment, and we do this by diligently studying the Bible, the book given to guide us in all matters of faith and holiness. "The life of discernment is, therefore, a Word-focussed [*sic*] and Word-directed life, which develops a Word-saturated mind."[5] John MacArthur says, "As we are obedient to what we know, our knowledge of the Lord and of his will increases and deepens. As we are faithful to the light, we are given more of this light."[6]

Many of the decisions we face in life are easily decided by looking to the Bible. We know that we must honor our marriage vows and not commit adultery; we know that we must obey those who govern us unless they compel us to disobey God; we know that we must attend a local church. Scripture is explicit in many areas. And yet there are other areas where the Bible has little explicit guidance. In these cases, we must proceed through sanctified wisdom, wisdom gained by studying the truth of God's Word and discerning what is true from what is false. There are some useful principles we can

---

[4]Sinclair Ferguson, *Let's Study Ephesians* (Edinburgh: Banner of Truth), 133 (emphasis in original).
[5]Ibid., 134.
[6]John MacArthur, *Ephesians* (Chicago: Moody, 1996), 210.

use to seek and follow God's will in matters that Scripture may not address directly:[7]

• Where God's commands are explicit, we must obey immediately, joyfully, and without question. We have no need to wrestle with issues that are addressed clearly in the Bible. Rather, we look to Scripture, understand what we must do, and do it immediately and without hesitation. While discernment may play a role in this, even a child or a new believer is able to understand most of what God has made explicit. We need only obey.

• Where the Bible contains no explicit guidance, God gives us freedom and responsibility to choose what we will do. We do not choose randomly or haphazardly but with prayer and reliance upon Scripture. We choose on the basis of what we know about the character of God and on the basis of the truth revealed through the Bible.

• Where the Bible contains no explicit command or guidance, God gives us wisdom and discernment to choose what we will do. It is here that we must exercise discernment. God gives us the gifts of wisdom and discernment so we can make decisions that honor him. With our knowledge of the truth we are equipped to make decisions that are consistent with his self-revelation. Exactly how we use discernment to make decisions will be the topic of chapter 10.

• When we have chosen what is moral and wise, we must trust the sovereign God to work all the details together for good. We are able to have confidence that God is faithful, and that he will reward us for making decisions based on the truth of his Word.

Note that nowhere do we attempt to discover and make decisions upon the basis of God's hidden will. We do not need to wait for a prophetic voice or inner promptings or a vision to guide us. We do not open the Bible at a random page and assume that it will guide us. Rather, because we are people who love and know and treasure the truths of God, we seek to live in a way that pleases him. We seek to prioritize what he prioritizes, and we seek to emphasize what he emphasizes. We obey the will of God as it is revealed to us

---

[7]This process is adapted in part from a process outlined in Garry Friesen, *Decision Making and the Will of God* (Sisters, OR: Multnomah, 1980).

in the Bible and thus have confidence that we are doing the will of God. Our hearts become so sanctified by God that we want nothing more than to do His will.

Christians sometimes speak of making "right" decisions. They speak of coming to a place where they need to make a decision and need to make the right one. But when we are living in God's will, obeying his will as it has been revealed to us, there are no right and wrong decisions. When we have ruled out what God has expressly forbidden, and when we have searched the Bible and prayed for wisdom, we are free to choose. This seems to be what is modeled for us in the New Testament. We do not find people desperately seeking God's will through dreams or visions (though occasionally God saw fit to use such miraculous means), but we see people making decisions based on what seemed good or best or necessary. We trust in the truth of the words of Proverbs 3:5–6, which read, "Trust in the LORD with all your heart, and do not lean on your own understanding. In all your ways acknowledge him, and he will make straight your paths." We trust in the Lord, we do not depend on our own flawed understanding of matters, and we acknowledge him. In this spirit the Lord will make our paths straight, and we will both know and do his will.

UNDERSTANDING AND OBEYING GOD'S WILL

Understanding and obeying God's will is not instantaneous. Because discernment is not given immediately and in full measure, understanding and obedience will require dedicated effort. Thankfully, as we have seen, the power and ability to discern are given at the moment of conversion, so we can have confidence that with effort even a new Christian can be discerning. All Christians must seek to understand and obey God's revealed will. We are not to concern ourselves unduly with the secret will, for we will never be able to know it fully or finally. "We should not be concerned with the sovereign will of God when we face a decision (except that we need to be ready to accept whatever the Lord has planned).

The guidance we need for our choices does not have to be

somehow mined from the mysterious and unknowable plan devised among the Holy Trinity in eternity past. Rather it is a relatively simple process of finding out what the Bible says and doing it."[8] We cannot and should not expect God to make known the full details of his plan before we follow in humble obedience. Obeying God's will is a relatively simple process of uncovering the truths of God so we might do the will of God.

Understanding and obeying God's will relate to the portion of our definition of discernment that speaks of "right from wrong." Discerning God's will, we could say, is the skill of understanding and applying God's Word with the purpose of separating right from wrong. It is discernment in a moral or ethical dimension in which we attempt to act in a way that is consistent with truth and that brings praise and glory to God. It is here that we live out what we believe. It is here that we will prove whether what we believe is accurate. If what we do and how we act is consistent with the will of God as revealed in Scripture, we can know that our beliefs are also consistent with the truths of the Bible.

We need to exercise discernment in knowing and obeying God's will whenever we encounter a situation in life that demands we make an important decision. When we encounter a crossroads in life we must examine the options available to us and make a decision that honors God. We rely on our knowledge of what is true about God to examine the paths stretching out before us, seeing which would lead us into error and which would lead us into truth. When we seek to discern God's will, we must always look back to what is true about God as he reveals himself in the Bible. Decisions are founded upon truth, so we do not usually look to see if a particular course of action is allowed or prohibited in Scripture. Rather, we look for the truth and the principles that the action is founded upon and take those back to Scripture.

As I write this, my sister and brother-in-law are contemplating moving to New York City. As they have approached me for my counsel, I have told them that they should not base their decision on what they perceive as open doors or feelings of internal peace.

---

[8]Dave Swavely, *Decisions, Decisions* (Phillipsburg, NJ: P&R, 2003), 51.

Rather, they should look for principles that would govern this move: will my brother-in-law be able to provide for the family in New York City, thus fulfilling his role as the provider? Will they be able to find a church where they can meet with God's people and serve among them? Do they have pure motives for wanting to move? Will this move be valuable in shaping them into Christians who love, trust, honor, and reflect God? I trust that these principles, these truths, will guide them to God's will.

D. A. Carson discusses another question about which answers are often sought from Scripture:

> Someone in the West may ask the question, "What does the Bible say about keeping fit?" The expected answers will be trotted out: our bodies are the temple of the Holy Spirit; bodily exercise may not profit eternally but does profit somewhat in this life; and in any case we are not dualists or Gnostics: *all* of life, including physical life, is to be lived under Christ's lordship. And at the consummation we will receive resurrection bodies. None of the answers is false. Our trawling has not been entirely without profit. But all the answers are skewed, in that the Bible does not set out to answer questions about keeping fit. Even at the tangential level it says things that may be relevant to the question *only within the context of larger, bigger questions* that are finally tied to God's plan of redemption and thus to God's priorities, God's purposes for his people.[9]

While the Bible does not speak to every issue, every issue will somehow tie into God's plan for the redemption of his people. This will in turn lead us to God's purposes and finally to God's will.

The twelfth chapter of Romans shows us that there are three stages to understanding and obeying God's will.[10] Though listed ordinally, they are in reality concurrent. These are not stages that are akin to grades in primary school. We do not progress from stage one to stage two, forever leaving the first stage behind as we would leave the first grade when we move to the second. Rather, these stages are

---

[9]D. A. Carson, *The Gagging of God* (Grand Rapids, MI: Zondervan, 1996), 545.
[10]This material is drawn in part from John Piper's sermon from August 22, 2004, "What Is the Will of God and How Do We Know It?" (http:desiringgod.org/Resource Library/Sermons).

interwoven and we should be working throughout our lives on all three stages concurrently.

The first stage is being transformed by having our minds renewed ("be transformed by the renewal of your mind" [Rom. 12:2a]). If we are to discern God's will, we must dedicate ourselves to knowing and understanding his Word as it is given to us in the Bible. In the Greek we read that our minds must be *metamorphousethe*, a word you will recognize as the root of the English *metamorphosis*. Just as a caterpillar undergoes a transformation, a metamorphosis, to become a butterfly, Christians must have their minds transformed. This word is elsewhere translated as "transformed" or "transfigured" and is used of Jesus when he appeared before his disciples at the transfiguration. This is the kind of change we are to undergo as Christians. We can only undergo this transformation by immersing ourselves in the Word of God. This stage of knowing the truth of God, while it comes first, will never end, for we must always learn more and more of him. The more we learn of God, the more we will *want* to know of God, and the more we will see that there is so much more to know.

The second stage is to begin to apply the truths we learn in the first stage to situations and decisions we encounter in life. There may be times when the Bible addresses a particular situation very directly and very clearly. In this case it is simple to know how to be obedient to God. But there will be other times where we need to do a great deal of work in attempting to understand God's will. It may become clear to us only with months of sweat and tears, and it may conclude in a leap of faith.

There are many areas the Bible does not address at all, and in these we need to exercise our best judgment and do so in accord with biblical principles. "What is necessary is that we have a renewed mind, that is so shaped and so governed by the revealed will of God in the Bible, that we see and assess all relevant factors with the mind of Christ, and discern what God is calling us to do."[11] Where God does not address an issue directly, or where the issue regards his secret will rather than his revealed will, we must not seek to hear his

---

[11]Ibid.

voice telling us what to do. We could easily find our lives brought to a standstill by attempting to discern why God has allowed a particular evil to befall us, or less importantly, whether we should wear a brown belt or a black one. Our discernment must be held to issues in which God has given us the ability to see and obey.

And so we use the truths contained in the Bible to bring clarity to the situations life brings. We do not seek new information from God; we do not seek fresh revelation but seek to apply the principles of the Bible to our decisions. We do so with confidence that the Bible is sufficient for all matters of decision, all matters of discernment.

And finally we come to the third stage. This is the stage where we live most of our lives, where we have little time or expend little effort in making choices or choosing our words. This is the vast majority of our time, when we speak without forethought and act without meditation. These are the times when we see what is inside of us, for our spontaneous thoughts and actions reveal a great deal about our hearts. Our conscience, through which we make so many quick decisions, is like a mirror reflecting what is in our hearts. It is "out of the abundance of the heart [that] the mouth speaks" (Matt. 12:34). And it is here that we will first see the results of the renewing of our minds. As our hearts and minds are renewed and transformed, they will bring forth fruit that is good and pleasing to God. Our spontaneous thoughts and actions are a sure measure of our spiritual growth, our spiritual maturity, and our spiritual discernment.

In this third stage we renew not only our minds, but our hearts and our emotions as well. Discernment does not affect only our willpower but also our emotions. We are to love and hate not as abstract decisions but as emotional ones. God's sanctification is to touch our emotions and make them hate what he hates and to love what he loves. When we laugh at what is evil or grow angry at what is good, we show that our emotions have not become discerning. We show that we need to continue to renew and transform our hearts.

As our hearts and minds are renewed, as we learn to distinguish between what is good and what is bad, we will find increasingly that our will and the will of God are one and the same. We will find joy and peace not in following our own path but in allowing our minds to be so changed that our desires are the same as God's.

> [I]n order to discern the will of God for their lives believers cannot just depend on their conscience. Conscience is indeed very important, but it must constantly be sent back to the school of Scripture to receive instruction from the Holy Spirit. It is in this manner that believers become and remain aware of God's will. Which will? Decretive [secret] or Preceptive [revealed]? The latter, of course. . . . In this way the will of God will become an increasingly well-established or proven component of the consciousness and lives of God's children. The more they live in accordance with that will and approve of it, the more also, through this experience, will they learn to know that will, and rejoice in that knowledge. They will exclaim, "Thy will is our delight."[12]

We are truly discerning in heeding the will of God when we can say with King David, no matter the situation, "I desire to do your will, O my God; your law is within my heart" (Ps. 40:8). With God's law in our hearts we can know the truth of God and thus delight in obeying him.

We use discernment, then, to distinguish between what is good and what is bad. We learn what God would have us do in a given situation by looking to the truths of the Bible and separating the options before us that are bad from the ones that are good. We use discernment to apply the truth of the Bible to the situations we face in daily life. Through discerning God's will we make decisions and act in ways that are shaped by what we believe to be true about God. We make decisions that honor him and bring glory to his holy name.

KEY THOUGHT

Once we know what is true about God, we can rightly know his will for our lives. We do not seek to know God's secret will but his

---

[12]William Hendrickson, *Romans* (Grand Rapids, MI: Baker Books, 1981), 406.

revealed will that tells us to be filled with the Spirit, to be sanctified, and to be thankful. And in honoring this will, we must exercise
discernment as we distinguish between choices that are consistent
with God's self-revelation and those that are not. We are truly discerning in obeying God's will only when we can say that his will is
our delight.

the GIFT of DISCERNMENT

*Beloved, do not believe every spirit, but test
the spirits to see whether they are from God, for many false prophets
have gone out into the world.*

— 1 JOHN 4:1

THOUGH I GREW UP ATTENDING CHURCH, my parents were never members of a congregation that had a youth leader. In fact, I have only one memory from my youth of interacting with such a leader. I was staying with a friend for a while, and we went to his church on a weekday evening for the church's youth meeting. The leader, who seemed so old to me, but who was probably only in his young twenties, had us play a game. He asked all of the kids to stand in a big circle and handed one of us a giant ball of yarn. The game was simple: we had to hold tight to the end of the wool, pay a compliment to one person in the room, and then toss that person the ball of yarn. The recipient was then to choose another person, pay him a compliment, and pass the yarn to that person. We were going to create a web of sorts. Of course, being teenagers, the compliments were not always heartfelt.

"I like your sweater," said one boy to another, and threw the wool at his head.

"That's a nice ketchup stain on your pants," said the next person, before lobbing the wool to the far side of the room.

Before too long, the ball of wool was reduced to a tiny nub, and there was a web of yarn as wide as the circle of bored teenagers. "Now, let's pull this apart," the leader said. We were now to reverse all we had done, attempting to unweave the web. This was impossible, of course. We could not remember who had thrown the yarn to whom. We tried, but the web just got more and more tangled. We gave up. "The moral of the story," said the youth leader, "is that so much love just can't be undone."

We were all disappointed by the moral of the story. Only a young, naïve, and idealistic youth leader could hope that we would be impressed by this little game. To tell the truth, I had completely forgotten about that evening until I began to write this chapter and began to ponder the gifts of the Holy Spirit, because like the web we spun with wool that night, the gifts of the Holy Spirit are meant to build within the local church a web of love and service that cannot be undone.

The issue of the gifts of the Spirit has, sadly, been a force for division within the church. This is both tragic and pitifully ironic, for the Spirit's gifts are given for the benefit and unity of the church. They are meant to bless and unify, not divide. And yet the church has seen a great deal of division along the lines of what different Christians believe about the gifts. Some Christians believe and teach that the miraculous gifts of the Spirit (prophecy, speaking in tongues, and healing) were given for a time but have since ceased. Others believe and teach that they continue, are operative in the church today, and need to be both sought and practiced.

Many theologians divide the spiritual gifts into two broad categories: those that are intended primarily to edify the church and those that are intended primarily to authenticate the Word of God. There is some disagreement among Christians today about whether this second category of gifts, the miraculous gifts, has ceased (hence the word *cessationist* to describe this group of people) or whether it continues (hence the word *continuationists* to describe the second group of people). I am grateful that this discussion is outside the context of this book and is, thus, not particularly relevant to our topic. There is much about which cessationists and continuationists agree, and our discussion conveniently falls within that area of agreement. Both groups can agree that God can and does dispense a gift of spiritual discernment.

SPIRITUAL GIFTS

The basic theology of spiritual gifts can be found in Paul's first letter to the Corinthians: "Now there are varieties of gifts, but the same Spirit; and there are varieties of service, but the same Lord; and there are varieties of activities, but it is the same God who empowers them all in everyone. To each is given the manifestation of the Spirit for the common good" (1 Cor. 12:4–7). This passage outlines several important principles regarding the gifts.

Variety

There are several passages in the New Testament where the author lists one or more of the spiritual gifts. It is interesting that, while there is some overlap, each list is unique and includes items that are not in each of the others. This seems to point us to the unavoidable truth that the gifts mentioned in Scripture are representative of the types of gifts God gives; they are not meant to serve as exhaustive lists. The variety of spiritual gifts is as wide as the variety of people whom God welcomes into his family.

The variety of gifts is meant to build a stronger church. The variety is not meant to disrupt the church but to unify it through diversity. "The church reflects unity in its totality but not uniformity in its parts. The church has been blessed with varieties of gifts that reflect diversity and contribute to unity."[1]

Empowered by the Spirit

Spiritual gifts are inherently spiritual for they are dispensed by the Holy Spirit. Christians today are often encouraged to seek out their spiritual gifts and to do so by way of spiritual gift assessments.

---

[1]Simon J. Kistemaker, *1 Corinthians* (Grand Rapids, MI: Baker Books, 1993), 418.

These assessments allow people to fill out a questionnaire of sorts and, on that basis, to discover how the Spirit seeks to work through them. Though these assessments may not be without any value, they do have at least one inherent flaw: they typically encourage people to seek out gifts by examining their personalities. Yet Scripture seems to show that the gifts of the Spirit may not necessarily be those that are strictly in accord with our personalities. The Holy Spirit dispenses gifts as he sees fit and, having done that, empowers their use.

In Everyone

To whom are spiritual gifts given? According to Paul, they are given to every believer. In the first two verses of 1 Corinthians 12 he writes, "Now concerning spiritual gifts, brothers, I do not want you to be uninformed. You know that when you were pagans you were led astray to mute idols, however you were led" (1 Cor. 12:1–2). Those who have been led away from worshiping idols, those who have been led away from paganism to the truths of God, have been given a spiritual gift. In other words, every believer without exception is blessed with a gift of the Holy Spirit.

Manifestation of the Spirit

There are two reasons that the Holy Spirit gives spiritual gifts. The first is so that his power and presence can be manifested in the church. When something is made manifest, it is made known or made visible. What was once invisible is now brought to light and becomes easily recognized. These gifts are meant to make us see and understand the work of the Spirit in the church and to lead us to glorify him and to make much of him. So here is one reason for spiritual gifts: to manifest the Spirit.

For the Common Good

There is a second reason that we are given spiritual gifts: for the common good. They are not given to be self-serving but to serve others. They are given for the common good, not for the individual

Christian. Thus when we exercise our spiritual gifts we are not to focus on ourselves or to marvel or cause others to marvel at our spiritual maturity or prowess. Rather, we are to serve other believers. John Piper ties these two purposes together in a beautiful way:

> This is right at the heart of our understanding of biblical theology: the pursuit of God's glory and the pursuit of what is good for us are not two separate pursuits. If you want to do good for people, you try to manifest God to them. If you want to manifest God and make him known for who he really is, you make it your aim to do good to others.[2]

One thing remains to be said about spiritual gifts. Even if we may not have been given a particular gift, this does not indicate that we are freed from our responsibility to practice it at least in some measure. We are not to pursue only one gift as if this is the only way in which God desires that we serve him. We are not to make a gift the most prominent aspect of our identity as Christians so that one member of the church becomes the "evangelism guy" and another member becomes the "hospitality woman." Just as the existence of a gift of evangelism does not preclude those who have not been given this gift from the task of evangelizing, in the same way, even those who do not have the spiritual gift of discernment are expected to be discerning. Still, there is a special place in the church for those who are gifted in discernment, and they have a special responsibility to practice their gift. We will now look at discernment in the context of spiritual gifting.

DISCERNMENT AS A GIFT

As soon as Paul has provided this basic theology of spiritual gifting, he lists some of the gifts of the Spirit. In this list he mentions a gift that provides "the ability to distinguish between spirits" (1 Cor. 12:10). Christians typically refer to this as the gift of discerning spirits. By now you ought to recognize the word *distinguish* as a word that is intimately related to discernment. In Greek it is *diakri-*

---

[2] John Piper , "Living in the Spirit and in the Body for the Common Good" (http://www.desiring-god.org/ ResourceLibrary/Sermons/ByDate/1992/818).

sis, a word closely related to *diakrino*, which was mentioned in the chapter "Defining Discernment." It is a word that indicates that we are to separate things in order to understand their differences. It is that word that is at the very heart of discernment. The gift involves "distinguishing between spirits."

The Bible does not elaborate on what this gift entails. Students of the Bible have to examine the evidence and determine what they feel this gift involved and whether it continues in that form to this day. One thing all students of the Bible seem to agree on is that there is some kind of gift of discernment operative in the church today. Yet the question remains: is the gift of discernment today the same as the gift of distinguishing between spirits as it existed in New Testament times?

I am not convinced that we need to solve this dilemma. Because the Bible makes it clear that there is great variety of gifts operative in the church, I see no reason not to suppose that discernment is one of these gifts. It seems clear that discernment is an issue that concerns God deeply, and it stands to reason that he would gift some people in this area. Whether the gift of discernment today is exactly the same as the gift of discerning the spirits in the early church may be beside the point. After all, the Bible does not describe the gift any further than simply listing it. When we look at Scripture and attempt to decide what this gift looked like at the time the Bible was written, we are, in the process of doing so, likely discovering how the gift operates today.

What Is This Gift?

The Bible makes it clear that, even in the church's infancy, there were many false prophets and teachers who claimed to speak God's words with God's authority. These men were strangers to God and yet claimed to speak for him. Many Christians were drawn in by their words and were led astray by them. Because of this, Scripture contains many exhortations for Christians to test all teaching. John writes, "Beloved, do not believe every spirit, but test the spirits to see whether they are from God, for many false prophets have gone out into the world" (1 John 4:1). Just one verse earlier, in 1 John 3:24, John has spoken of the fact that the Holy Spirit is given to us as evidence of God's presence in our lives. And having spoken of the Spirit, John now ensures that his readers know that not every spirit is holy. We are tempted to believe and obey spirits, for they represent a spiritual realm that is outside of our experience, but many spirits are commanded by Satan, the father of lies. Because of this we need to test or prove the spirits to see if they come from God.

Some commentators draw a direct line from the spiritual gift of prophecy to the gift of discerning spirits, but I am not sure this argument can be sustained. When we combine the presence of this gift with Paul's exhortation to "test everything," it seems that the gift of discernment would be likely to extend far beyond prophecy.

All Christians are responsible to test words of teaching and prophecy. The Bereans were considered noble for hearing the teaching of Paul and Silas, receiving them with eagerness and "examining the Scriptures daily to see if these things were so" (Acts 17:11). These believers tested the words of the apostles, examining the Scriptures to see if what they were being taught was consistent with what they knew of God's revelation of himself. In doing this they modeled the task of all believers. Christians are ultimately responsible for what they choose to believe, no matter whether or not they have been gifted with the spiritual gift of discernment.

While all Christians are responsible for what they believe, it seems clear that some people are especially gifted by God for this task. This is not merely a gift, but a responsibility. "Certain difficult cases occur, for which more than common Christian discernment is necessary. False prophets love to use deceptive language. For the purpose of unmasking these prophets the Lord provides this gift and thus enables his church to turn from lying spirits to the one Spirit of truth."[3] The gift of discernment is the Spirit's special defense against the lies that come from lying spirits.

The power and influence of spirits can be discerned in word, deed, and appearance.[4] Satan communicates in *words* that are

---

[3] R. C. H. Lenski, *The Interpretation of 1 and 2 Corinthians* (Minneapolis: Augsburg, 1963), 504.
[4] Simon Kistemaker, *1 Corinthians*, 524.

inconsistent with Scripture and that convey information we know to be false. This happened when Satan approached Eve and directly contradicted what God had told her (Gen. 3:4). It happened when Jesus rebuked Peter for denying that he would die, saying, "Get behind me, Satan! You are a hindrance to me. For you are not set-ting your mind on the things of God, but on the things of man" (Matt. 16:23). Jesus discerned that behind Peter's voice was the spirit of Satan. And so every word about God or that supposedly comes from God must be carefully tested and examined in light of the Bible.

As Satan and his spirits communicate in word, they also com-municate in *deed*. Just as Jesus was able to perform miracles, so Satan and his minions are able to perform signs and wonders. Second Thessalonians 2:9 warns that "the coming of the lawless one is by the activity of Satan with all power and false signs and won-ders." In the last days, Jesus warns, "false christs and false prophets will arise and perform great signs and wonders, so as to lead astray, if possible, even the elect" (Matt. 24:24). Deeds, no matter how extraordinary and how beneficial they appear, must be examined and compared to the Word of God.

Satan and his spirits can be discerned in *appearance*. Satan invades the Christian community with teachers and leaders who counterfeit the truth. These people will always introduce teaching that is foreign to Scripture. In Acts 16, Paul and Silas are met by a slave girl possessed by a spirit of divination. For many days she fol-lowed the apostles crying out, "These men are servants of the Most High God, who proclaim to you the way of salvation" (Acts 16:17). Though her words were true, the spirit behind them was false and sought to lure people with a little bit of truth so that the opportunity could be used to heap reproach upon the gospel. Paul judged her words to be true but knew by appearance that the spirits guiding her were insincere. He was not fooled by what might have been an appearance of godliness. And so appearances must also be carefully weighed against the Scriptures.

Men and women with the gift of discernment are specially gifted in distinguishing between those words, deeds, and appearances that are true and those that are false. John MacArthur summarizes the implications of the gift of discernment in this way:

> It can be said that the gift of discernment is given to tell if the other gifts are of the Holy Spirit, if they are merely natural imitations, or if they are demonic counterfeits. I believe God still empowers some of His people to unmask false prophets and carnal hypocrites. He gives them insight to expose imitations and deceptions that most Christians would take as genuine.[5]

Those Christians who are gifted with discernment will be able to compare ungodly words, deeds, and appearances with what God has revealed in Scripture and expose the fraudulent leaders and teachers for what they are. They are gifted with unusual ability in separating what is true from what is false and what is right from what is wrong.

How Do I Know If I Have This Gift?

The Bible seems to indicate that Christians will typically know how they have been gifted. There is certainly nothing that would hint at the modern methods of discovering gifts through surveys or assessments. And yet, while most Christians know that the gifts of the Spirit are given to God's people, they continue to struggle with identifying the ways in which God has gifted them.

Because gifts are given for the benefit of the body, it seems likely that where there is a need, there will be someone with the gifting to fill that need. If a church has a desperate need for a person with the gift of teaching, it seems likely that someone within the church has been given such a gift and may fill the need, at least for a season. Similarly, if a person is a member of a church where there is no opportunity to exercise a certain gift, it may be that this church needs to create opportunities for that; in extreme cases, the person needs to seek a church where his gifts can be of service to others. The leaders of churches should seek to ensure that they are providing opportunities for members to exercise the full spectrum of gifts.

---

[5]John MacArthur, *1 Corinthians* (Chicago: Moody, 1996), 305.

Wayne Grudem writes, "Though the lists of gifts given in the New Testament are not exhaustive, they certainly provide a good starting point for churches to ask whether at least there is opportunity for *these gifts* to be used."[6]

For those who continue to struggle with identifying how they have been gifted, here are five principles that will prove helpful:

Begin with Prayer

God promises to give wisdom to any who ask for it. "If any of you lacks wisdom, let him ask God, who gives generously to all without reproach, and it will be given him" (James 1:5). Thus we should begin our search for gifting by asking God to make it plain to us how he has gifted us and how he desires that we serve him by serving others. We must ask for wisdom in seeing how God has gifted us and in opening our eyes to opportunities to serve him.

Look for Passion

Where God has given a gift, we can expect that he will also give passion. A good place to begin when considering spiritual gifts is to see where God has given desire and passion. A person who is passionate about having people into her home may well have a gift of hospitality; a person who loves to organize events may be gifted with a kind of leadership; a person who is passionate about the truth of God may be gifted with discernment. Those who look for their gifting should look to what interests them and what makes them feel passionate. As they look to their passions they may just find their gifts.

Ask Others

Another way of seeking gifting is to ask other believers, especially those in spiritual leadership over you. Simply ask other Christians, those who know you best and who lead and guide you, where they feel you should serve within the church. Ask them to prayerfully consider your gifting. Their wisdom and guidance may surprise you.

---

[6]Wayne Grudem, *Systematic Theology: An Introduction to Biblical Doctrine* (Leicester: Inter-Varsity Press, 1994), 1028.

Try Them!

Christians should try different opportunities to serve within the church. As we attempt different things and do so in the power of the Holy Spirit, we can expect that he will reveal passion and gifting in ways we may not expect. There is a danger in doing only those things that we are comfortable with or serving only in the ways we think we are most talented. Think of Moses, a frightened and timid man being called to lead a nation, or the apostle Paul with a thorn in his flesh being called to take the gospel to all the nations. God does not always gift us in ways we are comfortable with or in ways we might expect. By attempting different gifts we can look to those where God brings blessing and success and perhaps see that we have a special gifting in these areas.

Keep Trying!

The Bible does not tell us that all spiritual gifts are given at the time of conversion or that, once given, they are given permanently. As we grow in our knowledge and love of the Lord, we should continue to seek ways of serving him. We may be surprised to find that our gifting changes along with the needs of our local church. We may find that God wishes us to emphasize different gifts now from those we emphasized in the past. So keep serving God and keep searching for his gifting in your life.

If confusion continues, take heart, wait patiently for God's wisdom and guidance, and serve him whenever and wherever possible. He will answer your prayers.

What Do I Do with It?

In his commentary on 1 Corinthians, John MacArthur makes the important point that the gift of discernment is especially necessary and especially valuable during those times that Christianity is considered acceptable in society.[7] When the church is enduring an era of persecution, there are bound to be few false teachers, for not many people are willing to risk their very lives for something they believe

---

[7]John MacArthur, *1 Corinthians*, 304.

to be false. The stakes are simply too high for such false teachers. But, as church history can attest, when Christianity is accepted and tolerated, false teachers arise quickly and soon fill the church. Those of us who are privileged to live in a nation that allows us freedom to worship must be particularly cautious. The truth is under attack more today than at any other time in history and this should not be surprising in a culture that so values religious freedom and tolerance. Add to such an accepting culture unparalleled speed of communication and the ability to publish books and other writings quickly and easily, and we can rightly conclude that error is being spread with startling speed and efficiency. What the church needs today is a class of believers who are identified as the experts in discernment and as those who have special ability in this area.

If we believe, as the Bible teaches, that spiritual gifts are given for the benefit of other believers, it seems clear that the purpose of the gift of discernment is primarily to protect other believers and to protect the local church. Where evangelism is a gift that is offensive in nature, taking the battle to new regions, discernment is a defensive gift that protects the ground that has already been taken.

In general, those with the gift of discernment should be able to identify and expose the spirit of Satan. While all believers are exhorted that they must "not believe every spirit, but test the spirits to see whether they are from God" (1 John 4:1), those with the gift of discernment have been given special ability and responsibility. They are equipped by the Spirit to expose the lies of Satan in the teaching of men. They are able to see to the heart of the issues and to see Satan's shadow behind what does not accord with the Word of God. Following are some specific and practical ways in which this gift can be exercised in the church today.

Separating Truth from Error

The theme of separating truth from error is a constant one in any discussion of discernment. The primary task in discernment, as we have seen repeatedly in this book, is to separate what is true from what is false. Thus the primary way a person with the gift of discernment can serve the church is to be a student of the Word and to use his understanding of Scripture to distinguish between what is true and what is false. It is the discerning person who will be comparing the words of the preacher with Scripture, and who will lead the way in warning others of false teaching.

Discerning the Will of God

We have learned already that discernment concerns first the truth of God and then the will of God. A person with the gift of discernment can assist others in seeking and finding the will of God. This must be done in a way that is consistent with the biblical principles outlined in the sixth chapter.

Identifying the Presence and Work of the Holy Spirit

People with the gift of discernment are finely tuned to the presence and the work of the Holy Spirit. They are able, based once again on their knowledge of God and the truths he has revealed about himself, to understand how he works and where he is working. They are also gifted in being able to tell where the Spirit is *not* present and in warning others of counterfeit teaching or counterfeit Christians.

Identifying Worldliness

Because the spirit of Satan breeds worldliness rather than godliness, men and women with the gift of spiritual discernment are able to see worldliness for what it is. Many Christians, and especially young Christians, confuse carnality for godliness, man-made rules for God-ordained holiness. Discerning Christians will be able to distinguish between what is truly holy and what is simply a manufactured holiness that leads only to failure and discouragement.

Overseeing the Exercise of Spiritual Gifts

People with the gift of discernment are able to oversee the exercise of other gifts, ensuring that they are done in a way that will bring honor to God and serve other believers. They are able to see when the exercise of gifts is inconsistent with Scripture.

Deciding Disputes

First Corinthians 6 finds Paul criticizing the church at Corinth for taking disputes between believers before the world. "Can it be," he asks, "that there is no one among you wise enough to settle a dispute between the brothers?" (1 Cor. 6:5b). What has been translated "settle a dispute" is the word *diakrino*. Most other translations say something like "judge a dispute between believers" or "judge between fellow believers." It may be that Paul indicates that believers who are gifted in discernment should lead in settling such disputes, using their knowledge of God's truth to judge or distinguish between what is right and wrong.

Protecting New Christians

Because discernment depends so much on knowledge of God's truth, Christians with the gift of discernment should place particular emphasis on protecting the young and the immature believers who have not had time and opportunity to grow in their understanding of the Bible. Those with the gift are able to surround and protect them, shepherding them by ensuring they are not led astray and leading them to greater understanding of what the Bible teaches.

Those Christians who are gifted in discernment have endless opportunities to serve God by serving the church. What I have listed here is only the beginning. Opportunities will be as wide and as diverse as the church itself.

What If I Want It?

The Bible tells us not only that we have spiritual gifts, but also that we are to desire spiritual gifts. There is no shame in desiring the gift of discernment or any other gift, as long as it is desired that we may use it to manifest the Spirit and to serve the body of Christ. However, we must be prepared that God may not see fit to answer this prayer. God may choose to gift us in ways other than what we would prefer, and we know that he will gift in ways that fill needs throughout the church.

If you desire this gift, ask God for it. Ask with expectation but with humility, knowing that God knows best and that he has so fitted the church together that you may need to be used in another way on the basis of another gift. And even if you are never convinced that you have been given this gift, practice discernment nevertheless!

What If I Don't Have It?

If you are certain that you have not been given the gift of discernment, find someone who has and ask that person for assistance when necessary. And no matter what, continue to seek to grow in discernment. Even if God has not specifically gifted you in this way, he still expects you to grow in discernment and to practice this discipline. Do so to his glory and for the benefit of the church.

Because of the sin and evil that lives within us, we are capable of turning any good gift into something that brings shame and disgrace. In our next chapter we will look at the potential dangers of discernment and see how this good gift can be twisted and perverted.

KEY THOUGHT

All Christians are given gifts of the Holy Spirit that serve to bring unity to the church by manifesting the Spirit and serving other believers. Among these gifts is the gift of spiritual discernment. People with this gift will have special ability to separate truth from error and to discern whether something originates with God or with Satan. There are a wide variety of opportunities to serve the church through this gifting. Even though not everyone has been given the spiritual gift of discernment, we are all to pursue this discipline.

the DANGERS of DISCERNMENT

*I want you to be wise as to what is good
and innocent as to what is evil.*

ROMANS 16:19B

THE PEOPLE OF CANADA arc losing confidence in their currency. Recent polls suggest that only a little more than 50 percent of Canadians have a good deal of confidence in their currency, while 39 percent believe it is likely that they would at some time receive a counterfeit bill. The Bank of Canada, the body responsible for producing and overseeing Canada's currency, reports that four one-hundredths of one percent of currency in circulation today is fraudulent. While that number may be small, it does prove that it is at least somewhat likely that a person will, over the course of his lifetime, encounter counterfeit currency.

The Bank of Canada, taking a proactive stance against this erosion of confidence, has embarked on a program of education, the goal of which is to help Canadian consumers and retailers regain their confidence by equipping them to distinguish between genuine and fraudulent currency. The Bank of Canada is teaching a form of discernment.

As we noted earlier, training in identifying counterfeit currency begins with studying genuine money. There are certain identifying characteristics that are added to each bill printed by the Bank of Canada. These characteristics are necessarily difficult to reproduce. Some are intended to stump the casual counterfeiter, armed with no more than a scanner and color laser printer, and some will stump the more serious counterfeiter, even if he is equipped with expensive, high-tech equipment. The approach to distinguishing a genuine bill is summarized with the phrase "touch, tilt, look through, look at."

The first step, then, is to *touch* the bill. Because currency is printed on unique cotton-based paper, a false bill will often feel false. The most common reaction to the feel of a counterfeit bill is that it is waxy. A person may not quite be able to describe it, but something about it just feels wrong. From long experience of handling genuine money, experts can often immediately identify a false bill simply by the fact that it feels wrong. There are also two areas on a bill where raised print provides a tactile clue to a genuine bill.

Having touched the bill, people are encouraged to *tilt* it. Each bill features a holographic stripe that is remarkably difficult to accurately reproduce. As the bill is tilted, this holograph will show all the colors of the rainbow. Additionally, each tiny maple leaf on the bill is color-split, so that, when the bill is tilted, the leaves appear in two colors simultaneously. Finally, when studied closely tiny numbers identifying the denomination of the bill will appear in the background of this stripe.

The third step is to *look through* the money. By holding a bill to the light, several features appear. There is a small, ghost-like watermark image of the bill's main portrait. In the case of a twenty-dollar bill, this means that a tiny portrait of Queen Elizabeth II appears immediately beside a more pronounced portrait. Another of these "look through" features is a gold thread woven through the bill that will appear solid when held up against a light source but broken or staggered if counterfeited.

The final step is to *look at* or study the bill. "Look at" features include fine-line printing within the bill's portrait and certain background patterns. These lines and patterns are so fine that they cannot be adequately reproduced by the casual counterfeiter. Even counterfeiters equipped with the latest equipment have a difficult time adequately reproducing this micro-printing.

Interested in discovering just how the bank hopes to equip Canadians to discern between currency that is genuine and currency that is fraudulent, I sought out an expert in the field and was soon invited to speak with one at the Bank of Canada's regional office. I was provided with a compressed version of the training provided to agents who are taught to seek out counterfeit currency.

After my introduction to counterfeit detection I found that my training would be put to the test. I was provided an assortment of bills of varying denominations, and I was told that some were genuine and some were counterfeit, having been confiscated by the bank. My task was to determine which were genuine and which were fraudulent.

The first bill I examined, a twenty-dollar bill, immediately struck me as a forgery. Just as I had been taught, it felt waxy and seemed to have been printed on standard pulp-based paper. I tilted it and noted that the holographic stripe was not holographic at all. Though I was already convinced that this was a forgery, I pressed on and noted that no portrait of the Queen appeared when the bill was held to the light, and the fine-line printing was blurry and imprecise. It was clearly and obviously a counterfeit, and a poor one at that.

The next bill was a genuine five-dollar bill. I examined it and found that everything seemed in order. The security features were in place, the print was sharp, and hidden features appeared just as they should. The bill felt just as I expect money to feel.

I continued to move through the stack of bills. One bill almost seemed sound, but upon close examination I noted the thinnest white edge on the bill, proving that it had been poorly cut from a sheet of white paper. I moved quite quickly through the money, examining each using the four tests I had been taught. I successfully identified each piece of counterfeit currency. I did not accept any of the frauds.

There were several lessons I learned at the Bank of Canada that are as easily applicable to spiritual discernment as they were to the battle against counterfeit currency.

First, it quickly became apparent that identifying counterfeit currency is not an exceptionally difficult task and certainly not one that only experts can master. When a person has been taught what to look for, when he has been trained to examine bills for particular identifying characteristics, identifying genuine from fraudulent can be done with great accuracy.

Second, I learned that people who create counterfeit money typically invest minimal effort in creating a reproduction of the genuine currency. Under scrutiny the fraudulent money is easily identified.

Third, I learned the importance of identifying a number of characteristics of truth. These characteristics will be present when something is true and will be missing when something is false. When discerning whether something is true or false, one would have to look at only a few characteristics to decide if it is genuine or fraudulent. What is fraudulent does not always need to be thoroughly examined; for certain identifying characteristics will ensure that truth and error are soon separated.

And finally, I learned that in discerning what is true from what is false it is best to focus more attention on what is genuine than on what is counterfeit. It would be tempting to train people to identify what is fraudulent by focusing a great amount of time on what is false. However, because falsehood is always changing, it is more beneficial to focus on what is unchanging. Knowing and identifying what is false can be done best by knowing and understanding what is true. A person who studies and understands what is true is necessarily equipping himself to discern what is false.

All of these lessons point us back to the fifth chapter of this book, where we looked at the importance of truth, the characteristics of truth, and the test of truth. But I want to invest just a bit of time in looking at this final point—that in discerning truth from error it is critical that we spend more time dwelling upon truth than upon error.

It is sad to say that the word *discernment* has negative connotations in the minds of many Christians and non-Christians alike, for those who claim to exhibit discernment are often those who lack love. Somehow the desire to defend the truth seems to overshadow the ability to exhibit love. Truth and love are brought into conflict rather than being equally present. And so, in this chapter, we'll look at ten of the potential dangers that seem to afflict those who emphasize discernment. We will see what can happen when discernment goes awry.

THE DANGERS OF DISCERNMENT

1) Innocent as to What Is Evil

Interestingly, the foundation of counterfeit detection taught by the Bank of Canada is the same as that encouraged by the apostle Paul, for he writes to the men and women of the church of Rome, "I want you to be wise as to what is good and innocent as to what is evil" (Rom. 16:19b). He wants these Christians to invest their time studying not what is evil but what is good. When they have confidence in all that is good, the evil will become ever more apparent.

This is not the first or only time Paul has given this exhortation. In 1 Corinthians 14:20 he wrote, "Brothers, do not be children in your thinking. Be infants in evil, but in your thinking be mature." And in saying this he echoes the words of Jesus, who exhorted his disciples and warned them of the persecution that would come, saying, "Behold, I am sending you out as sheep in the midst of wolves, so be wise as serpents and innocent as doves" (Matt. 10:16).

> Here Paul is warning against wolves in sheep's clothing—people departing from the doctrine who talk like sheep and bless like sheep but "do not serve our Lord Christ." They are wolves ready to devour the naïve. When it comes to wisdom—the discerning of false teaching and destructive behaviors—don't be naïve. Be wise; be mature. But when it comes to evil—erroneous destructive doctrines and appetite-worship that goes with them—be innocent. Be like a child in the sense that you don't even make a beginning in evil. J. B. Phillips paraphrases Romans 16:19, "I want to see you experts in good, and not even beginners in evil.[1]

---

[1]John Piper, "The Peace of God Will Soon Crush Satan Under Your Feet" (http://www.desiringgod.org/ ResourceLibrary/Sermons/ByDate/2006/1881).

There is a danger inherent in the practice of discernment. Those who seek to draw clear distinctions between what is good and what is evil can spend undue time and attention on the evil. One of the greatest dangers of discernment is that we will become so interested in what is evil and ungodly that we allow ourselves to become immersed in it and inadvertently oppressed by the evil we encounter.

But the Bible commands that we are to be innocent as to what is evil. As John Piper warns, we are not to even make a beginning of evil. Our efforts in discernment should revolve around knowing the truth so that we might see the evil in contrast to what is true. The reason it is better to focus on what is true is simple: error is constantly changing, shifting, and morphing into new forms, always seeking to imitate what is true in new and creative ways. Truth, however, is constant. When we know what is true we will more easily be able to identify what is error.

2) Guilt by Association

In my experience the most prevalent danger of discernment is falling into the trap of guilt by association. This is not only a spiritual fallacy but also a logical one. It is a kind of association fallacy which posits that a property of one person must be true of another simply because they are in some way associated. It is also known as the "company you keep fallacy" or the "bad company fallacy." In a spiritual context it teaches that someone or something must be wrong or false simply because of the people that support it. It may take this form: Pastor Smith believes that Jesus is not God. Pastor Jones mentioned Pastor Smith's book in a sermon once. Therefore, Pastor Jones does not believe that Jesus is God. The guilt of Pastor Smith has been applied to Pastor Jones because of some perceived relationship between them. This is a fallacy because it is unfair and illogical to suppose that a relationship between two people, whether it is a friendship or merely a mention in a book or sermon, is a blanket endorsement of all a person writes or teaches.

Guilt by association is a trap people fall into when they are lazy in their discernment. Rather than understanding the beliefs of a particular individual and comparing those to the Word of God, they judge the person based on the beliefs of another person. They irrationally associate the guilt of one person's poor theology onto another.

3) Honor by Association

The flip side of guilt by association is honor by association. This is likewise illogical when it comes to spiritual matters. Where guilt by association conveys the idea that someone or something must be wrong because of the people who support it, honor by association conveys that someone or something must be right because of who supports it. In this way we can overlook the transgressions of people we like simply because of our respect for them. We may also respect people or their teaching simply because of the teachers they ally themselves with.

The fallacy may take this form: Pastor Jones believes the Bible shows that a particular doctrine is wrong. Pastor Mitchell, though, teaches that this doctrine is biblical. He studied under Pastor Harrison, who Pastor Jones regards as a great teacher of the Bible. Therefore Pastor Mitchell must be right and this doctrine must be biblical. The honor accorded to one person has overruled the biblical admonition to test everything.

Like guilt by association, honor by association is a trap people fall into when they are lazy in their discernment. Instead of comparing the beliefs of a particular individual to the Bible, they judge a person's credibility based on the beliefs of another. They irrationally associate their approval of one person on the basis of their approval of someone else.

4) The Critical and the Disputable

Another danger of discernment is ignoring the fact that some doctrine is of greater importance and greater urgency than other doctrine. Al Mohler makes the insightful observation that lowering the status of first-level doctrine to the level of disputable matters is the cause of liberalism, while elevating third-order doctrines to the status of first-order is the cause of fundamentalism (see chapter 4 for the discussion of first- second- and third-order doctrines).

The error of theological liberalism is evident in a basic disrespect for biblical authority and for the church's treasury of truth. The mark of true liberalism is the refusal to admit that first-order theological issues even exist. Liberals treat first-order doctrines as if they were merely third-order in importance, and doctrinal ambiguity is the inevitable result.

Fundamentalism, on the other hand, tends toward the opposite error. The misjudgment of true fundamentalism is the belief that all disagreements concern first-order doctrines. Thus, third-order issues are raised to a first-order importance, and Christians are wrongly and harmfully divided.

A man or woman of discernment will not allow the foundational doctrines of the faith to be lowered to the level of disputable matters. Likewise, a discerning person will not allow matters of lesser importance to ascend to positions of utmost importance.

5) Witch Hunting

It seems from Scripture that discernment is largely a defensive posture, one that waits for error to rear its ugly head and reacts to it in a measured and deliberate fashion. There may be times when Christians feel the need to go looking for error, and there may be people who can serve the church by rooting it out, but more often than not, there is enough error in the world that we do not need to seek it out deliberately. As we have seen, there is a danger inherent in focusing a ministry on seeking out error. Focusing our efforts in discernment in seeking out the smallest transgression will lead to spiritual oppression.

As I was discussing this topic with a friend, he shared with me this little pearl of wisdom: "Those who witch hunt end up riding brooms." Sooner or later, Christians who spend their days seeking out and responding to the transgressions of other people can quickly become insufferable. The spiritual oppression inherent in continually seeking out what is evil begins to take its toll. Their attempts in discernment somehow lead them to forsake discernment.

The book of Proverbs has much to say about such people—about those who cause discord in the church:

> A worthless person, a wicked man,
> 	goes about with crooked speech,
> winks with his eyes, signals with his feet,
> 	points with his finger,
> with perverted heart devises evil,
> 	continually sowing discord;
> therefore calamity will come upon him suddenly;
> 	in a moment he will be broken beyond healing.
>
> There are six things that the LORD hates,
> 	seven that are an abomination to him:
> haughty eyes, a lying tongue,
> 	and hands that shed innocent blood,
> a heart that devises wicked plans,
> 	feet that make haste to run to evil,
> a false witness who breathes out lies,
> 	and one who sows discord among brothers. (Prov. 6:12–19)

God regards it as a grave offense when Christians cause discord within the church, destroying the church's unity. While unity cannot be emphasized at the cost of the gospel, it can also not be forsaken because of the slightest disagreement. A person who continually stirs up anger and disagreement is committing an offense that the Lord hates.

6) Relying Unduly on Others

There is danger in relying on other people's discernment and especially that of people we don't know. The most natural context for discernment is the local church, where issues particular to a congregation can be dealt with. Those charged with discernment are known to be godly, discerning people. When we go looking to books and the Internet as our primary source of discernment, we risk being unduly influenced by people who are not truly discerning. We risk exposing ourselves to people who seek to destroy rather than edify, and who are, perhaps inadvertently, heaping scorn upon the church. We need not look far to find countless examples of Christians who were simply curious and looking for information about a teacher or doctrine but were led into all manner of false doctrine by seeking out discernment through books or web sites. There are many people in the Christian world eager to do anonymously the work of discernment for us. Sadly, it seems that few are suited to the task.

7) Simplicity

It is easy, when attempting to be discerning, to neatly categorize people into two camps: safe and unsafe or good and bad. We then implicitly trust the people in the good camp and entirely reject anything said by those in the bad camp. To do so, though, is to ignore the common grace God gives whereby even those whose views are far different from our own can still be wise and can still speak the truth. While we need to read their words with care and discernment, we can and often should still read their words. We need to rest in the security of the Spirit's guiding and protecting ministry in our hearts rather than in sheltering ourselves from views that do not always accord with our own.

Dennis E. Johnson, professor of practical theology and academic dean at Westminster Seminary California, warns his students against this error:

> We cannot simply compile a list of "safe" authors, stamp them with the Reformed equivalent of *imprimatur* or *nihil obstat*, and then confine our reading to them. We must do the hard work of exercising discernment—sentence by sentence, paragraph by paragraph, argument by argument. Facts, insights, perspectives, and methods must all be tested in the light of the principles of Scripture. And we must keep alive our consciousness of dependence on Christ, in whom are hidden all the treasures of wisdom and knowledge. Our safety is not in avoiding the ideas of the unbelieving world; our safety is in union with Christ, who transforms the mind of those who trust in him.

There is hard work to be done in sorting and sifting the teachings of other humans, especially when we realize that we cannot
simply cubbyhole the unpleasant or challenging ideas away and
ignore them. But this hard work, like other exercise, gives us the
necessary muscle tone to serve and lead God's people. "Solid food
is for the mature, who by constant use have trained themselves to
distinguish good from evil" (Heb. 5:14).[2]

As we mature in our faith, and as we gain discernment, we will see
how the hard work of being discerning, even about teaching that is
not consistent with Scripture, has helped us attain maturity.

8) Pride

Those who emphasize discernment seem to be particularly prone
to the sin of pride. As their discernment increases, and as they
become able to separate more consistently what is true from what
is false, they can sometimes become proud of their abilities. They
may begin to crave recognition as a discerning person and may
desire that the results of their efforts make them look strong and
spiritual rather than lifting high the name of Jesus. They can even
make discernment into an idol, giving glory to their own discernment rather than to the God who is both the source and motive of
all true spiritual discernment. Those who wish to be discerning can
and must emphasize humility, a topic we will discuss in more detail
in the next chapter.

9) Withdrawal

A. W. Pink was a Christian theologian with a prominent ministry
during much of the early twentieth century. Gifted as a teacher and
pastor, his desire to find a place to worship where he agreed with
everyone and everything eventually led him to leave the church
altogether. He could find no church where he could worship or
participate in good conscience and with full support. And so he
withdrew from participating in a church, secluding himself and his
wife. In doing this he denied the church a great teacher, did not use

---

[2]Dennis E. Johnson, "Common Grace and Theological Scholarship" (http://www.wscal.edu/
faculty/ wscwritings/commongrace.php).

his gifting to bring blessing to the church, and removed both himself and his wife from Christian fellowship. While he sought to be discerning, he actually disobeyed the Bible's command that we remain in the fellowship of a local church.

There are some legitimate reasons for leaving a particular church body, but it is rare that the better alternative is to not join any church at all. Christian fellowship is an integral part of the Christian life and one that we are not free to ignore. And yet many people who emphasize discernment find themselves increasingly unhappy in their local churches and may soon find themselves hiding away, either participating only grudgingly or attempting to replace church with sermons on CD or downloaded from the Internet. But discernment does not give us license to ignore Christian fellowship and to separate ourselves from other believers. A discerning person will know and affirm the value of the local church, of accountability, and of Christian fellowship. He will heed the words of Hebrews 10:24–25: "Let us consider how to stir up one another to love and good works, not neglecting to meet together, as is the habit of some, but encouraging one another, and all the more as you see the Day drawing near."

10) Truth without Love

Perhaps the greatest danger in discernment is that it can be done from poor motives. Discernment can be done out of anger, a contentious spirit, a critical heart, or a desire to cause disagreement. When our discernment is driven by poor motives it will become a negative, critical discipline rather than a positive, uplifting one. We need to see discernment as an opportunity to defend what is right and to serve other Christians. It is wise to examine our hearts and see whether we are being discerning out of good motives or selfish, unbiblical ones.

We will close this chapter, a chapter that has been largely negative as we have looked at what can happen when discernment goes awry, by affirming the importance of right motives. As we seek to practice discernment, God tests our hearts. "Just as we have been approved by God to be entrusted with the gospel, so we speak, not to please man, but to please God who tests our hearts" (1 Thess. 2:4). Like Paul, we should be overwhelmed with the desire to please God so that when he tests our hearts, our inner beings, he will see that our hearts and motives are pure and that we seek only to bring him praise and glory. Our efforts in discernment should proceed from hearts that are pure—hearts that desire to build up, not destroy. John Stott speaks of the importance of speaking truth in love:

> Thank God there are those in the contemporary church who are determined at all costs to defend and uphold God's revealed truth. But sometimes they are conspicuously lacking in love. When they think they smell heresy, their nose begins to twitch, their muscles ripple, and the light of battle enters their eye. They seem to enjoy nothing more than a fight. Others make the opposite mistake. They are determined at all costs to maintain and exhibit broth-erly love, but in order to do so are prepared even to sacrifice the central truths of revelation. Both these tendencies are unbalanced and unbiblical. Truth becomes hard if it is not softened by love; love becomes soft if it is not strengthened by truth. The apostle calls us to hold the two together, which should not be difficult for Spirit-filled believers, since the Holy Spirit is himself "the Spirit of truth," and his firstfruit is "love." There is no other route than this to a fully mature Christian unity.[3]

These are wise words that lead us to the heart, which is the very heart of the matter. We are to speak the truth in love (Eph. 4:15), a love first for God and his truth but also a love for a brother or sister in Christ. We must not allow our eagerness to defend truth to overcome our love for our brothers and sisters in Christ. This is clearly a danger for those who are discerning, and one we would do well to consider.

Having looked at the dangers of discernment, we'll turn next to the Bible's teaching about how we can develop discernment in a way that will avoid these pitfalls and bring glory to God.

---

[3]John Stott, *The Message of Ephesians* (Downers Grove, IL: InterVarsity, 1979), 172.

KEY THOUGHT

Because of our fallen natures, discernment is a practice that can lead to many dangers. While the Bible exhorts us to focus on what is good and to be innocent as to what is evil, many people who seek to be discerning inadvertently practice a counterfeit discernment that is merely a shadow of the real thing. There are many traps awaiting these people. Spiritual discernment is a matter of the heart and must be done with a pure heart and for pure motives.

chapter nine

DEVELOPING DISCERNMENT

*And it is my prayer that your love may abound
more and more, with knowledge and all discernment,
so that you may approve what is excellent.*

PHILIPPIANS 1:9–10

ROY HALLADAY IS THE Toronto Blue Jays' ace pitcher and is one of the top players in baseball. Halladay has a well-established routine that begins as soon as a game is complete and continues until the next game has begun five or six days later. He has another routine that takes him from the end of one season to the beginning of the next. And, like many players, he has a routine that takes him from pitch to pitch. His off-season regimen, which prepares him for a long and grueling season of baseball, is legendary, and it readies more than his arm. To prepare his mind he reads *The Mental ABC's of Pitching* seven or eight times every season. To hone his concentration he carries with him a series of laminate grids filled with a hundred randomly numbered squares that he crosses off in order, from 00 to 99, with an erasable marker. "Every day that I'm not pitching, I'm doing something that's going to help me when I'm out there, not just vegging on the bench or in the hotel room," he says.[1]

---

[1]Cathal Kelly, "Halladay: A Master of Detail" (http://www.thestar.com/Sports/article/190739).

To prepare his body he works out constantly and vigorously so that he rarely breaks into a sweat during a game. He has the reputation of being the team's hardest worker. Not surprisingly, he is also the team's best player. His team members flock to him, eager to learn from his routine, so they, in turn, can become better players. While Halladay is clearly a talented athlete, what sets him apart is his preparation. He prepares to pitch with rigorous physical and mental effort. He tends to more than his arm, but looks to his entire body and mind. He knows that to be a great player requires skill and preparation in a wide variety of disciplines.

Similarly, the pursuit of spiritual discernment is not an isolated pursuit. Discernment is not something that is available or that can be attained apart from other disciplines of the Christian life. In this chapter we will examine some related pursuits and some important prerequisites to discernment. Just as a person who wishes to win a race will have to begin the race in a certain posture—crouched low with legs ready to spring forward—a person who wishes to be discerning must maintain a particular spiritual posture. This chapter discusses the spiritual posture of a discerning Christian—the daily, life-long pursuits that will allow him to grow in discernment.

THE COMMITMENTS FOR DISCERNMENT

The second chapter of Proverbs begins with the type of statement that should be quite familiar to those who have read and studied the Old Testament. It is a simple "if . . . then . . ." statement. Similar to the covenants God made with his people, there is a promise and an obligation. There is a simple correlation between the two pieces of the statement. If several conditions are met, results will follow:

> My son, *if* you receive my words and treasure up my commandments with you, making your ear attentive to wisdom and inclining your heart to understanding; yes, *if* you call out for insight and raise your voice for understanding, *if* you seek it like silver and search for it as for hidden treasures, *then* you will understand the fear of the LORD and find the knowledge of God. (Prov. 2:1–5)

In these verses we see the lifelong commitments that will enable us to be men and women who both pursue and display discernment.

Pursue Discernment

First, we see that we must be actively involved in the pursuit of discernment, for we are to receive the words that are given to us. We are to treasure up the commandments, making our ears attentive and inclining our hearts to understanding. We must prepare ourselves by ensuring we meet the prerequisite for wisdom in fearing the Lord. As we learned already, only those who fear the Lord have any hope of attaining wisdom and discernment. We must also exhibit humility before God, knowing that without divine wisdom we are hopeless and helpless. We need to see in ourselves the need for wisdom and the need for discernment. We need to be aware of our own foolishness and must earnestly desire to have that foolishness put aside. And we must exhibit humility before men, allowing the wisdom of God to come to us through people he has chosen. The means may be Scripture. It may be a teacher, a pastor, or a parent. In Proverbs 2 it is Solomon, who brings in his words only so far as he is convinced that these are God's words. He has taken the law of God and, by faith and obedience, made it his own.

Desire Discernment

Second, we see that we must passionately desire discernment. We need to pursue wisdom as a treasure. Just as we would passionately seek after hidden treasure, we must seek after insight and discernment. We must value it as being much greater and much nobler than any amount of wealth. We've seen this outlook modeled by Solomon himself. If you recall, we noted that after God offered Solomon any desire of his heart, Solomon, still just a young adult, cried out, "Give your servant therefore an understanding mind to govern your people, that I may discern between good and evil, for who is able to govern this your great people?"

We cannot expect that wisdom and discernment will be immediately bestowed upon us in full measure. It is likely that even

Solomon was not given full wisdom and discernment in a moment, but rather that God gave him extraordinary ability to pursue wisdom and to grow in discernment.

Pray for Discernment

Third, we must pray for discernment. We call out for insight and understanding by crying out to God, admitting our failures to discern and humbly asking that he will help us do better in the future. We ask God, who sees all things exactly as they are, to grant us his insight and clarity. We rely on him to equip us and to empower us. We see the importance of prayer in Paul's letter to the church at Philippi: "It is my prayer that your love may abound more and more, with knowledge and all discernment, so that you may approve what is excellent" (Phil. 1:9–10). Paul prayed that God would bestow discernment to these people.

Seek Discernment

Finally, we must seek discernment. We pursue knowledge and wisdom and discernment by pursuing the Word of God. A person who wishes to be discerning will necessarily and always be a person who commits to reading and studying the Bible on a regular basis. It will be a person who is motivated to study the Bible, individually as well as in the context of a local church.

THE CONTEXT FOR DISCERNMENT

In his wisdom, God has ordained that Christians are not to be isolationists and are not to hide themselves away in private enclaves. Rather, Christians are to participate in spiritual communities and are to be accountable to one another. The local church is provided by God as a means of grace and as the context for much of the personal growth that Christians experience. The local church is the Christian's most natural context in which to learn, to model, and to practice spiritual discernment. It is also the context in which we can learn tolerance toward others and learn to understand which issues are worthy of great attention in our attempts to be discerning and which are not. We learn tolerance, we learn to live peaceably with others, and we learn to serve others through the local church.

Asaph, who authored at least twelve of the psalms, provides an example of the role of the church in discernment in Psalm 73. This song begins with Asaph feeling downcast, considering how he nearly stumbled after becoming envious of ungodly men who were able to prosper despite their sinful lives. But by the grace of God he was able to keep from stumbling.

> But when I thought how to understand this,
> it seemed to me a wearisome task,
> until I went into the sanctuary of God;
> then I discerned their end. (Ps. 73:16–17)

When Aspah went to the house of the Lord, seeking God in the Word and in prayer, God helped him discern how wicked men will come to ruin. God showed that the treasures of this life are fleeting, and that he is a treasure far greater than anything this world can offer. These two verses are the turning point of the psalm, the point where it moves from despair to praise. By meeting with the Lord and his people, Asaph's hope is restored, and he leaves the sanctuary praising God.

In his book *Nine Marks of a Healthy Church*, Mark Dever provides five reasons that Christians must join a church:

1) For assurance. While a person should not feel he *needs* to join a church in order to be saved, he ought to join a church to be *certain* that he has been saved. Christians, those who are indwelt by the Holy Spirit, will naturally gravitate towards other Christians and will desire to be with them, to learn from them, and to serve them. A person who professes Christ but feels no desire to be among his believing brothers and sisters is not a healthy Christian. Thus, eager participation in a local church and heartfelt attempts to measure our enthusiasm for that group of believers is a God-given way for us to assure ourselves that we are truly saved.

2) To evangelize the world. The gospel can best be spread

through combined and collaborative efforts. Throughout the history of the church great men and women have attempted great things on their own and have often been successful. But more often, great things have been accomplished through the collaborate efforts of Christians working together. If we are to reach this world with the gospel message of Jesus Christ, we must share our efforts with other believers.

3) To expose false gospels. As we interact with other believers, we will see what true Christianity is, which ought to expose the common belief that Christians are self-righteous, selfish individuals. As we labor, fellowship, and serve alongside other Christians, and as we observe the lives of other Christ-followers, we will see what biblical Christianity looks like. The more we see of genuine Christianity, the more the counterfeits will be exposed.

4) To edify the church. Joining a church will help Christians counter their sinful individualism and teach them the importance of seeking to serve and edify others. The benefit of being a member of a local church is not primarily inward, but outward. Christians attend a local church so they might have opportunities to serve others and thus to serve God. Every Christian should be eager to serve within the church and to edify others through teaching, serving, and exercising the spiritual gifts.

5) To glorify God. We can bring God glory through the way we live our lives. God is honored when we are obedient to him. He is glorified when his people come together in unity and harmony to find assurance, to evangelize the world, to expose false gospels, and to edify one another. God is glorified in and through the local church.[2]

A person who wishes to grow in discernment must belong to a local church and must place himself under the authority of godly leaders. He must seek to help others grow in their knowledge and application of Scripture. The local church is the best, most natural, most biblical context for spiritual discernment. Discernment intersects with each of the five reasons we must belong to a church,

---

[2]Mark Dever, *Nine Marks of a Healthy Church* (Wheaton, IL: Crossway Books, 2004), 151–59.

and the church will be a more pure reflection of Jesus Christ when discerning believers are committed to it.

THE CHARACTER FOR DISCERNMENT

Discernment does not always come naturally. Because we are sinful and rebellious by nature, we are drawn to what is evil. We often hesitate to make judgments and distinctions lest we draw unwanted attention to ourselves or cause schisms with other believers.

A person who wishes to be discerning must be a person of humility. Discernment cannot flourish where there is a haughty or arrogant attitude. Humility must be seen in two ways.

1) Humility before God

First, and most importantly, we must be humble before God. We must acknowledge our own sin and our need of his grace. We must acknowledge our need for discernment, the insufficiency of our wisdom, and our lack of ability in applying wisdom to discernment. John Calvin says that Christians "are drunk with the false opinion of our own insight and are thus extremely reluctant to admit that it is utterly blind and stupid in divine matters."[3]

There must be a humble admission that the Bible is the very word of God, and that it will teach us all we must know. As the prophet Isaiah wrote millennia ago:

> "But this is the one to whom I will look:
>   he who is humble and contrite in spirit
>   and trembles at my word." (Isa. 66:26)

Reflecting on these words, C. J. Mahaney writes, "Humility draws the gaze of our Sovereign God."[4] Mahaney defines *humility* as "honestly assessing ourselves in light of God's holiness and our sinfulness."[5] When we consider God's holiness and our sinfulness, we must be led to acknowledge our absolute and utter dependence on God. We are sinful creatures, blind to what is good except

---

[3]John Calvin, *Institutes of the Christian Religion* (London: Westminster John Knox, 1960), 278.
[4]C. J. Mahaney, *Humility: True Greatness* (Sisters, OR: Multnomah, 2005), 19.
[5]Ibid., 22.

through the illumination of the Holy Spirit. And so we must cry out to him to give us wisdom and to give us discernment. As we humble ourselves before God, he will turn his gaze to us. As we cry out like Solomon did, asking for wisdom and discernment, God will surely answer, and he will surely provide.

2) Humility before Men

While humility before God is absolutely critical, it is not enough. We must also be humble before our fellow man. A person who desires discernment must acknowledge that he needs the assistance of other believers to help him grow in knowledge, wisdom, and discernment. He must acknowledge that the Christian life is not meant to be lived in isolation, but it is to be lived with a view to the diversity of the personalities and gifting of other Christians. He must choose to follow discerning leaders and to read books that are discerning in what they teach and in the resources they use. He must choose to surround himself with discerning people and to invite their encouragement and correction. He must always remember that "whoever walks with the wise becomes wise, but the companion of fools will suffer harm" (Prov. 13:20).

A person who wishes to be discerning must continually examine his motives, ensuring that he is motivated to protect not only himself but also his brothers and sisters in Christ. He must be motivated to be discerning so he can protect Christian brothers and sisters from blundering into error. He must also be willing and eager to address other people's error with humility and in a way that is consistent with Christian character. He needs to be motivated to teach others the importance of discernment, to model discernment, and to help others practice it. This all relies on humility.

Having acknowledged his own sin and inability, he must also be willing to hear reproof and to be challenged by others. He must know that there will be times when his sin overcomes his desire and ability to be discerning. During these times he must invite and heed the correction of other Christians. This will surely test his humility and show just how much he desires to be truly discerning.

MEEKNESS

The Christian who is humble must also be meek. Meekness is a gentleness that allows us to express humility in our dealings with others. A meek person will be very careful in how he reacts to lack of discernment in others. It is a gentle attitude and a gentle behavior. This does not mean that we may not react strongly and securely. We do not need to be scared or shy to speak out. However, we must act in a way that builds up rather than tears down. We must be both truthful and loving.

COMPASSION

We must have compassion for other Christians, knowing how easy it is to be led into error. Discernment based on compassion will cause us to see what it is we appreciate about others rather than simply causing us to tear them down. We will always be aware that we are all prone to stumble, and that we have fallen into all manner of error in our lives. It is only the grace of God that allows any of us to overcome the darkness that lurks within us, which constantly seeks to overtake us.

THE CONFIRMATION OF DISCERNMENT

The confirmation of discernment, the proof that a person is discerning, is found in obedience to the Bible. Discernment is more than a mere mental judgment about truth or error. Discernment requires a response; it requires obedience. Proverbs 28:7 says, "The one who keeps the law is a son with understanding." A person with wisdom and discernment is a person who obeys God's laws. Psalm 119:100 says, "I understand more than the aged, for I keep your precepts." The NET Bible provides a more literal translation: "I am more discerning than those older than I, for I observe your precepts." The proof of the psalmist's discernment is in his obedience to the laws of God. The verses that are foundational to this book, verses you will know well by this point, exhort Christians to "test everything; hold fast to what is good. Abstain from every form of evil" (1 Thess. 5:21–22). It is simply not enough to test doctrine. We must also respond in godly fashion to truth or error. This is so important that we will devote the next and final chapter to it.

Further proof is to be found in maturity, for as we saw in chapter 1, "A Call to Discernment," those who mature in their Christian faith are necessarily those who are increasing in discernment. Those who can be counted as discerning Christians are those who are obedient to the truth revealed in Scripture, and who are growing and maturing in their faith.

What we find is that if we are to pursue discernment, we must pursue God. We become discerning Christians not by focusing on discernment as an end in itself, but by focusing on the person of God and the character of God. As we pursue God, seeking to know him as he has revealed himself in the Bible, we necessarily grow in both wisdom and discernment.

We have seen the commitments and context of discernment; we have seen the character necessary for discernment, and we have looked at the proof of discernment. Having looked at these critical qualities, we will turn in the next chapter to the actual practice of discernment.

KEY THOUGHT

Discernment is not a pursuit that stands on its own in the life of the Christian. Rather, it is inexorably connected to others. Those who wish to be discerning must have a posture of discernment. They must commit to reading and studying the Bible, to participating in the local church, and to pursuing the character traits of a Christian. The lives of these people will display the proof of discernment in their obedience to the Bible and in their maturity as Christians.

chapter ten

the PRACTICE of DISCERNMENT

Test everything; hold fast what is good.
Abstain from every form of evil.
1 THESSALONIANS 5:21–22

IN THIS CHAPTER I will lead you step by step through the practice of discernment. So grab a pen and a couple of sheets of paper or open the word processor on your computer, and we'll get to work.

We are nearing the end of our study of discernment, and by this time you must be familiar with the clear similarities between the battle to prevent counterfeit currency from polluting our nations' economies and the battle to prevent counterfeit doctrine from polluting the church. Like separating genuine from counterfeit currency, the practice of discernment is simple. It involves a test that will bring about one of two reactions. We have already looked at the words "test everything" and have spent the better part of a chapter discussing what these words mean. We learned that we are to test every matter that is in any way relevant to the Christian life. This means that when we encounter a new teaching or come across an important decision in life, we must test. And once we have tested, we will need to react. The two possible reactions—hold fast and abstain—are the subject of this final chapter.

While the Bible provides a framework for the method of discernment, we will not find a verse or passage that explicitly instructs us point-by-point. Still, by studying the complete testimony of Scripture, it soon becomes apparent that God has not left us without instruction in this matter. People who are new to the practice of discernment may have to work through these steps very deliberately. However, with practice the steps will quickly become much more natural. A person who has long sought to be discerning will find himself moving easily from one step to the next, likely because he has been practicing these steps all along without realizing it. As you sharpen your skills of discernment, you will doubtlessly adapt these steps to fit your own style.

If the subject of discernment is still new to you, it may prove beneficial to seek out opportunities to practice discernment. To do this, you could simply read a Christian book or listen to a sermon. You could turn on the television to a Christian channel or tune in to a Christian radio station. You could listen to any teacher of the Bible, and it would not take long for you to find something that requires you to exercise discernment. You could also think back to times in life that you were faced with a decision in which you sought to know and do the will of God. Whatever the issue, it may prove helpful to keep it in mind as you move through this chapter.

ACTION 1: VERIFY

Write down a statement you would like to verify by the Bible such as:

- "I have to forgive God for the bad situations I have encountered in life."
- "The Bible tells me that I have to pray a prayer of forgiveness in order to be saved."
- "God is unable to know beforehand the decisions I will make."

As a case study, we will examine the idea of self-forgiveness. Some time ago I heard a song called "Forgive Yourself." It was written and performed by a Christian band and sought to teach the importance of self-forgiveness. Here is a portion of the song's lyrics:

Can you tell me how you spend every day
Looking in the mirror of your shame
And staring like a judge, you are ruling for yourself
You tied a stone around your neck
You're drowning in a past regret

Don't believe it's okay to be like this
Don't believe you deserve to live like this
'Cause every part of you wants to know
Just one reason why you should let go

Forgive yourself, forgive yourself
Nothing ever frees you more than just believing
Come out of the prison
You've been delivered

This song introduces the concept of forgiving yourself. To create my statement I will write, "The Bible teaches that we must forgive ourselves for past sin."

Prepare

The first step in discernment is ensuring adequate preparation. When you encounter a teaching or doctrine that requires discernment, there are two questions you will want to answer immediately: What is being said? and What is at stake? These are important questions, ones you will want to grapple with before proceeding any further. Consider what it was that disturbed you, gave you pause, or somehow made you uncomfortable. Consider *why* you feel this is a teaching or decision that requires discernment. It may be useful to write down your thoughts so that you can recall them later.

Ask What Is Being Said

This may seem obvious, but be sure you understand the issues at the very foundation. An important prerequisite for discernment is to ensure that you fully understand what is being said. It is far too easy to react immediately and violently without ensuring that you understand exactly what the other person has been saying.

As you seek understanding, make sure that you do not become distracted by the details but instead you see what is truly at the heart of the issue. The Pharisees were famous for missing the proverbial forest for the trees, often criticizing Jesus and his disciples for their innocent actions, all the while missing the more important issues relating to Jesus' person and mission. We need to ensure that we probe to the very heart of the issue rather than being distracted as the Pharisees so often were.

ACTION 2: CLARIFY

Write down your understanding of the issue at hand. Include both your understanding of the issue and the opposing understanding you have gleaned from another teacher. Applied to our case study, we might write the following:

> The song above teaches the idea of self-forgiveness. The song's lyrics indicate a person who is suffering from guilt or depression because of past sin and suggest that the solution to overcoming this is to forgive oneself on the basis of God's forgiveness. In other words, since we have been delivered from our sin by God, we should now forgive ourselves to free ourselves from the prison of guilt.

Ask What Is at Stake

As you ponder a teaching or doctrine, be sure to look beyond the surface and look to the ultimate. Determine what possible truths from Scripture could be violated by the idea you are considering. It is helpful to seek to understand what is assumed rather than made explicit. Does it fall within the first-order doctrines and violate a doctrine that is absolutely fundamental to Christianity? Is it a second-order doctrine that could potentially disrupt the unity in a local church? Is it a third-order doctrine—a disputable matter that would have little bearing on church unity and the foundations of the faith? This will give you perspective on the importance of this issue and its possible ramifications.

ACTION 3: ASSESS THE ISSUES

Write down what issue may be at stake. Determine just how important this issue is. Is it a first-order doctrine, a second-order doctrine, or third-order doctrine?

Assess Importance

This definitely does not appear to be a first-order doctrine, as it does not deny the fundamentals of the faith. It would likely be a second- or third-order doctrine. At stake is a sound understanding of the origin and importance of forgiveness.

Your preparation is now complete. You should have a sense of the importance of this doctrine and know just what is at stake. When you have ensured your preparation is complete, you are now ready to test.

Test

When we test a teaching, we distinguish between what is good and evil, separating truth from error and seeking points of departure. If an expert in counterfeit currency is uncertain whether a suspicious bill is genuine or counterfeit, he is able to compare it to one he knows is good. He can return to the standard and compare one to the other. In the same way, we can compare any teaching to the standard of Scripture and see how they compare. The Bank of Canada tells Canadians to "look through" a bill to see if it is counterfeit. By holding it up to a light source, features embedded in a genuine bill will show clearly. The small, ghost-like watermark image of the bill's main portrait will appear, as will a gold thread woven through the bill. The light source shines through, exposing what is fraudulent and highlighting what is genuine. And in the same way we can hold up a doctrine or a decision against the light of God's Word and allow this light to prove what is genuine and expose what is counterfeit.

We must test all things by holding them up to the light. This may seem like a long and laborious process. Sometimes it will be. No one claimed that discernment would be easy! It requires dedicated effort, and this is where you will learn just how much effort can sometimes be involved.

Pray

You must begin with prayer, for in so doing you will acknowledge your dependence upon God in the process of discernment. You will acknowledge that as the very author of truth, God is the one who must guide you, who must empower you, and who must be the one you seek to please. He is the source and power of discernment, and you must affirm your reliance upon him.

ACTION 4: PRAY

Proceed no further until you have prayed. Admit your dependence upon God in all matters of discernment and in understanding the truth of Scripture. Ask him to guide you now:

> Father, help me as I seek to discover what your Word says about forgiveness. I depend upon you to open my blind eyes and to unstop my deaf ears so I can hear your voice and see your glory in the Scriptures. Guide me to your truth that I may bring glory and honor to you. Amen.

Examine Your Instinct

Note whether your mind or heart immediately reacted with acceptance or with hesitation. While we cannot always trust our first reactions, experience shows that God does seem to wire us in such a way that our first instincts are often correct. This is especially true when we have immersed ourselves in the Bible and have attained some level of Christian maturity. You would not want to make decisions on this basis alone, but it still can play an important role overall.

ACTION 5: ASSESS YOUR INSTINCT

Write down your first instinct on this topic and why you feel this way, for example, "My first instinct is that self-forgiveness is not a biblical concept."

Listen to Conscience

While conscience is by no means an infallible guide, it can be valuable, particularly as Christians mature and their conscience is made increasingly tender through the work of the Holy Spirit. Scripture warns against violating the conscience, because acts that are taken against conscience cannot arise from faith. Thus, in our practice of discernment we must be attuned to hearing and heeding the conscience. It is useful to search your conscience and to understand if conscience is prohibiting you from accepting a belief or decision.

ACTION 6: ASSESS YOUR CONSCIENCE

Write down what your conscience is telling you. Does it feel right and good to proceed or does it nag your conscience and make you uncomfortable? So, for our case study we might write:

> My conscience tells me that self-forgiveness is not found in the Bible. I would be in violation of my conscience if I were to forgive myself in an attempt to be free from guilt for sins I've committed in the past.

Test with Scripture

Children learn by doing—they can only discern if something they find lying on the floor is good to eat by putting it in their mouth. Thankfully, as Christians we do not actually have to experience something in order to know if it is true or false, good or evil. God has given us his Word as the standard by which we are to gauge whether something meets his approval. We test a doctrine or teaching not by immediately embracing it, but by comparing it to the unchanging standard of Scripture. There may be times that you do not need to go through all of these steps. Sometimes the answer will become apparent long before you have worked your way through each of them. While instinct and conscience are important, they are not nearly as important as Scripture. Scripture is the perfect and holy standard, and it is here that we will be able to gauge whether our instinct and conscience are right.

In this step we gather a list of Scripture verses relevant to the subject at hand. We start with *observation*. Observe what Scripture teaches.[1] Begin by searching the Bible to find passages relevant to your question. You can do this simply by reading the Bible, by calling to mind passages you already know, or by using tools such as dictionaries, concordances, or the cross-references in your Bible. As your knowledge of Scripture increases, you will find yourself increasingly able to remember passages relevant to your study, and you will have an easier time doing this research. What may be laborious at first will, with practice and growing skill, become easier.

ACTION 7: SEARCH THE SCRIPTURES

Search your Bible for relevant passages and make a list of them. In terms of our examination of self-forgiveness, the Bible has a great deal to say about forgiveness. Here is a short list of some of the most relevant passages.

> Blessed is the one whose transgression is forgiven, whose sin is covered. Blessed is the man against whom the LORD counts no iniquity, and in whose spirit there is no deceit. (Ps. 32:1–2)

> And whenever you stand praying, forgive, if you have anything against anyone, so that your Father also who is in heaven may forgive you your trespasses." (Mark 11:25)

> Bearing with one another and, if one has a complaint against another, forgiving each other; as the Lord has forgiven you, so you also must forgive. (Col. 3:13)

> If we confess our sins, he is faithful and just to forgive us our sins and to cleanse us from all unrighteousness. (1 John 1:9)

> My little children, I am writing these things to you so that you may not sin. But if anyone does sin, we have an advocate with the Father, Jesus Christ the righteous. (1 John 2:1)

---

[1]These steps are drawn largely from Richard Mayhue's excellent little book *How to Interpret the Bible for Yourself*. Though it is out of print, it is still widely available on the Internet from used booksellers. I highly recommend it.

When you have found a list of relevant passages, move through them one-by-one. Observe each one individually.

Observe singularly. Look first to the Bible and do not move to other resources until you have read the passage repeatedly and meditated upon it. It is easy to short-change this step by moving immediately to others' interpretations, but do not give in to this temptation.

Observe carefully. Do not rush, but look long and look carefully at the passage in question.

Observe thoroughly. Look not only to the verse or verses that concern you, but also to the wider context of the passage and the book. Much can be learned by looking to context.

Observe systematically. Heed the advice of Martin Luther, who said, "First I shake the whole tree, that the ripest may fall. Then I climb the tree and shake each limb, and then each branch and then each twig, and then I look under each leaf." Begin with verses that discuss the subject in the broadest terms and from there move to verses that discuss it in greater detail.

Observe intimately. Read with the mindset that you are receiving a message from your heavenly Father to you, his child. Read with the knowledge that God desires to teach you from his Word.

ACTION 8: OBSERVE THE SCRIPTURES

Observe each passage prayerfully asking God to reveal his truth to you. Remember, at this time we are still looking only at individual passages and not at the wider topic. Write down a few words summarizing what you have learned from each of the passages. Having done the steps, outlined above, I have written a few words for each of the passages, outlining what each teaches about forgiveness or self-forgiveness.

- "Blessed is the one whose transgression is forgiven, whose sin is covered. Blessed is the man against whom the Lord counts no iniquity, and in whose spirit there is no deceit" (Ps. 32:1–2). There are blessings in store for a person whose sins have been forgiven *by God*.

- "And whenever you stand praying, forgive, if you have anything against anyone, so that your Father also who is in heaven will forgive you your trespasses" (Mark 11:25). We are to forgive *each other* so that God will continue to forgive us.

• "Bearing with one another and, if one has a complaint against another, forgiving each other; as the Lord has forgiven you, so you also must forgive" (Col. 3:13). We are to forgive *each other* as a way of modeling the forgiveness God extends to us.

• "If we confess our sins, he is faithful and just to forgive us our sins and to cleanse us from all unrighteousness" (1 John 1:9). When we confess our sins *to God*, he is faithful to forgive and cleanse us.

• "My little children, I am writing these things to you so that you may not sin. But if anyone does sin, we have an advocate with the Father, Jesus Christ the righteous" (1 John 2:1). When we sin, Jesus Christ stands as our advocate before the Judge.

Once you have collected the verses, you will need to understand what they say and what they mean. It may help to compare several sound Bible translations to see the difference in words (as I have done in this book, often noting where one translation uses the word *discernment* when another uses a synonym such as *insight*). While it is best to stick with a single, primary translation, other good translations can prove helpful in bringing to light particular nuances of language and translation.

ACTION 9: COMPARE AND CONTRAST

If certain passages seem unclear, compare them with another passage of Scripture from a good Bible translation. Write down any clarifying comments. In terms of self-forgiveness, we might write:

> Mark 11:25 was further clarified by a few of the alternate translations. For example, the Holman Christian Standard Bible makes explicit that we are to forgive others. "And whenever you stand praying, if you have anything against anyone, forgive him, so that your Father in heaven will also forgive you your wrongdoing."

By this time you should have a sense of which verses are most relevant to your inquiry. You may have found that some have no connection with the topic at hand, and these can be put aside. If you still have a long list of verses, choose a few that seem to be most relevant.

Investigate

When you have observed all you can from the passage, it is time to investigate what others have discovered. You will be amazed at just how much can be mined from a single passage. Turn now to your resources—Bible dictionaries, commentaries, and sermons. You may also wish to use a study Bible or to turn to a friend, pastor, or elder for assistance.

ACTION 10: RESEARCH

Turn to your Bible reference tools to see what others say about the passages you have found. Write down a few lines for each. Applied to our investigation of self-forgiveness, we might say:

> Space precludes me from writing about each of these passages. Suffice it to say that searching my Bible reference tools was a valuable process that yielded a bounty of clarifying information.

Interpret

Having observed and investigated, you now have what you need to properly interpret the passage. You will answer the question, "What does this mean?" Assume that the Bible should be interpreted as you would interpret any other book (including this one!). Take into account figures of speech and symbolism, but know that God has not made the Bible deliberately difficult or impossible for us to understand. Look to the whole of Scripture to ensure that the interpretation you draw from one passage is consistent with the rest of the Bible.

ACTION 11: SUMMARIZE

For each passage write a sentence or two summarizing what it means. Having done all of this, you should have a clear sense of what Scripture says about the topic at hand.

Seek Consensus

After we have prayed, examined conscience, and examined Scripture, we may find it helpful to seek the consensus of other Christians, in particular the consensus of the Christian church through the ages. Rarely does controversy arise that has not arisen in the past. Many of the doctrines we wrestle with today are the same ones Christians have wrestled with for two thousand years, which is why we turn to books and articles that can guide us. We search for teaching from discerning Christian leaders to learn what conclusions they have reached on a particular topic and, as importantly, the Scripture passages upon which they based their conclusions.

We may need to head back to Scripture ourselves, back to observation, investigation, and interpretation, to ensure that these people are correct. As time goes on, you will learn which leaders are discerning, which tend to teach what is consistent with Scripture. But always you must ensure that what they teach is biblical. Even the best of Christians will still be wrong at times.

ACTION 12: EXPAND YOUR RESEARCH

Search for books, articles, sermons, and other resources by discerning Christians. Note their conclusions and the Scriptural basis for them. In searching other resources on self-forgiveness, I was able to locate some material on this subject written by Bible-based, discerning authors. It is interesting that much of the material advocating self-forgiveness is written from the perspective of a New Age talk-show Christianity. This sort of Christian psychology tends to advocate the view that we need to forgive ourselves. One discerning leader who has written on this subject, though only briefly, is John MacArthur. He writes the following:

> I realize there are some who teach that a kind of self-forgiveness is necessary. I find this nowhere in Scripture. I've met many people who claim to be unable to forgive themselves, but on careful examination this usually turns out to be a kind of sinful pride exacerbated by modern self-esteem philosophy. The person who complains about not being self-forgiving is often simply looking

for flattering or consoling words from others as a way of salving the hurt that guilt has caused to their pride.[2]

MacArthur also quotes Jay Adams, who, in his book *From Forgiven to Forgiving*, writes:

> The problem is not self-forgiveness. Their expressed agony stems from the very fact that, in the worst way, they want to forgive themselves. They want to put it all behind them, they want to bury it once and for all. . . . The problem is that people who talk this way recognize something more needs to be done. Forgiveness is just the beginning; it clears away the guilt. They also recognize that they are still the same persons who did the wrong—that though they are forgiven, they have not changed. Without being able to articulate it, and using instead the jargon they have heard all around them, they are crying out for the change that will assure them they will never do anything like it again. When, as a counselor, I help them to deal with the problems in their lives that led to the wrong, in such a way that they lead a more biblical lifestyle, I then ask, "Are you still having trouble forgiving yourself?" Invariably, they say no.[3]

Hold It Up to the Light

We now have the evidence we need. We have looked at our instinct and conscience and have compared a doctrine or a decision to the Bible and to the consensus of the church.

ACTION 13: CONCLUDE

Write your conclusion about the issue at hand. For our case study, we can say:

> As we peer into Scripture, looking at these verses and others, it becomes quickly apparent that "forgive yourself" is not biblical language. There does not seem to be any place in Scripture where we are told to forgive ourselves, either in those words or even in concept. We are told to seek forgiveness from God and from our

---

[2]John MacArthur, "Answering the Hard Questions about Forgiveness" (http://www.gty.org/resources.php?section=positions&aid=197).
[3]Jay Adams, *From Forgiven to Forgiving* (Amityville, NY: Calvary, 1994), 25.

fellow man. We are told to extend forgiveness to those who have wronged us and release any bitterness we feel towards them. But it does not seem that we are ever told to forgive ourselves.

What Are the Points of Agreement?

We now know what we believe about the issue, but we still must think about how we will react. Return to the issue and look first for areas in which the Bible agrees with what has been said or done. These points of agreement can be useful in discussion. They are useful for beginning discussion on common ground before moving to the points of departure.

ACTION 14: MAKE A LIST

Write down a list of points on which the true and the false teaching agree. We would agree that forgiveness overcomes guilt. We would agree that we need to be forgiven. We would agree that not only do we need God to forgive us, but we also need to forgive each other. If I were to discuss this issue with another person, I would likely begin our discussion by affirming this common ground.

Are There Points of Departure?

We now look for potential points of departure. Just as counterfeit money bears a certain resemblance to genuine money, what is false often bears a passing resemblance to what is true. What we need to do is to seek out the point of departure, that portion of the teaching that begins the path that inevitably leads further and further from what is good and true. Once a doctrine has veered away from truth, it will not return but will carry on its trajectory until it does not look like truth at all. If we were looking for counterfeit money, we would look for missing watermarks, poor-quality printing, and other sure signs of something that is fraudulent. With the spiritual, we look for ways in which it departs from God's Word. While most doctrine will typically follow the Scripture for a while, any false doctrine will depart at one point or another. And this is the point we need to identify. This is the point we seek to find. Search for this point.

ACTION 15: JUDGE

Jot down the point at which the false teaching departs from the truth. Assemble all the evidence and make a judgment. Write down your conclusion. The point of difference in our study seems to be in the understanding of whom we sin against. The Bible teaches clearly that first and foremost, no matter who has been harmed by our sin and how many people have been affected by it, our sin is primarily sin against God. Many of those who advocate the view that we must forgive ourselves seem to have a low or nonexistent understanding of the holiness of God. Thus, in their view, our sin is primarily against ourselves; we do not need God in order to receive self-forgiveness. The view holds forth a selfish, self-centered perspective of sin that says, "Against myself, myself only have I sinned." It seems to me, then, that self-forgiveness has roots buried more deeply in self-esteem and sinful, human-centered psychology than in Scripture. Self-forgiveness and Scripture diverge at the point at which we identify whom we ultimately sin against.

It must be noted that while Scripture does not explicitly forbid self-forgiveness, it also does not require it or endorse it. It seems, then, that we do not *need* to forgive ourselves, nor should we make this our practice. If we struggle with guilt or shame, forgiving ourselves may be a temporary salve, but it cannot bring the peace and healing we seek. We can only have true peace, lasting peace, by accepting God's forgiveness and allowing him to remove the guilt of our transgression. This must be an act of God rather than an act of self, because true forgiveness will be found only in the very source of forgiveness.

By now, the most difficult task is complete. We have examined a suspicious doctrine or a difficult decision and have found whether it is true or false, right or wrong. We have separated truth from error and right from wrong, and we now have no choice but to take one of two options. There is no ambivalence. There is never a case where we can shrug our shoulders and walk away without taking any action. The results of our test are in, and we must act. The Bible makes clear not only the fact that we must act but also *how* we must act. We can abstain or we can hold fast. If a teaching has proven to be true, you can pass over the next step of "Abstain" and move directly to "Hold Fast." If the doctrine has proven to be false, you must work through both.

Abstain

When our test has shown a doctrine to be false, we must abstain from it. Our primary concern in this step is answering the question, "What do I need to abstain from?" We must abstain from every form of evil, every kind of evil. This passage is sometimes translated as "every appearance of evil," but this word, *appearance*, can be deceptive. After all, Jesus often appeared to be acting evilly when he dined with the Pharisees and met with other sinners. Though others charged him with sinfulness, he was blameless. What some thought was sin was not sin at all, though it may have had such an appearance. Avoiding the very appearance of sin does not necessarily insinuate that we should shun sinful people or avoid situations that may appear sinful to others. Rather, we must avoid things that have the appearance of evil because they actually are evil.

> *Evil* refers to something that is actively harmful or malignant. Such evil, which includes lies and distortions of truth as well as moral perversions, appears in many forms. Because of its many manifestations . . . the apostle warned the Thessalonians to shun "every form of evil." Paul's exhortation was a general call for believers to discern truth from error, good from evil, righteousness from sin, and a command to shun any of the negative teachings, influences, or behaviors that would displease God.[4]

We are to understand that evil assumes many different forms, and we are to ensure that we avoid whatever forms evil may take.[5] The Greek word the apostle used here, which we translate as "abstain," implies that we are to hold ourselves away from what is wicked. We are not to flirt with it or attempt to mold it to our

---

[4]John MacArthur, *1 & 2 Thessalonians* (Chicago: Moody, 2002).
[5]R. C. H. Lenski, *The Interpretation of St. Paul's Epistles to the Colossians, to the Thessalonians, to Timothy, to Titus and to Philemon* (Minneapolis: Augsburg, 1961), 362.

image. Rather, we are to cast it off, to cast it away, and to distance ourselves from it. Just as Paul told Timothy to flee youthful lusts, to run from them, we are to flee what is evil.

The Amish are infamous for their practice of shunning those who have fallen into sin and broken their baptismal vows, in which they promised faithfulness to God and his laws. When a person is shunned, members of the community refuse to associate with him. They will turn their back to him, eat separately from him, and refuse to acknowledge him. They will act as if he does not exist at all. The word *abstain* can also be translated as "shun," and in the Amish practice of shunning we see a picture of avoiding and abstaining from evil.

It must be noted that nowhere does the Bible give us permission to toy with evil. We do not need to invest a great deal of effort in knowing and studying false doctrine (though there may be exceptions among some individuals who are called to this kind of ministry). But we must take care that we do not give undue time and attention to that which is evil. John MacArthur writes:

> Scripture does not give believers permission to expose themselves to evil. Some people believe the only way to defend against false doctrine is to study it, become proficient in it, and master all its nuances—then refute it. I know some people who study the cults more than they study sound doctrine. Some Christians immerse themselves in the philosophy, entertainment, and culture of society. They feel such a strategy will strengthen their witness to unbelievers. . . . But the emphasis of that strategy is all wrong. Our focus should be on knowing the *truth*. Error is to be shunned.[6]

How we abstain from what is evil will vary from person to person and situation to situation. Abstaining may involve putting down a book or even throwing it away. It may involve ceasing to listen to a particular band, turning off the television, or not watching a movie. Joshua Harris encourages us to be "people who write in book margins, talk to our televisions, and discuss movies and concerts with

---

[6]John MacArthur, *Reckless Faith: When the Church Loses Its Will to Discern* (Wheaton, IL: Crossway Books, 1994), 79.

one another afterwards to help sharpen our discernment and to increase our ability to critique unbiblical values."[7]

If the teaching we examine is unbiblical, we must abstain from it. We should note what we found wrong with a teaching and what the Bible says about this. And here we come to the important principle of substitution. We must not just abstain, but we must dig deeper to understand what the truth is and substitute what is true for what is false. We do not end with rejection, leaving a void. Rather, we end with affirming, reaffirming, or embracing the flipside of the error. For every error there is an opposite truth. And so we move to the step called "Hold Fast."

ACTION 16: HOLD FAST

If a doctrine or action was shown to be unbiblical, write down what it is that you will abstain from. The lesson I draw from our case study is that we must always remember and believe that we sin primarily against God. What we need to avoid is a man-centered approach to sin where we first ask, "How have I harmed myself with this sin?" Rather, we must turn to God and ask him to forgive us, because our sin has been primarily against the Lord. We would err if we were to substitute self-forgiveness for true repentance before God and acceptance of his forgiveness. And thus we abstain from forgiving ourselves and relying on our acts, deeds, and words of penitence to make ourselves feel better about our sin. We abstain from downplaying the seriousness of our sin and the gravity of defying God and his laws.

While we are to flee what is evil and wicked, we are to hold fast to that which is good. The predominant concern in this step is answering the question, "What do I need to hold fast to?" One commentator notes of the word *good* that it "has a fine flavor in the Greek and means excellent, fair, and beautiful, something that is an honor and a grace to the possessor."[8] This is not a good that inhabits the little multiple-choice circle between fair and excellent,

---

[7] Joshua Harris, "Like to Watch" (http://www.boundless.org/2005/articles/a0001258.cfm).
[8] R. C. H. Lenski, *The Interpretation of St. Paul's Epistles to the Colossians, to the Thessalonians, to Timothy, to Titus and to Philemon*, 363.

but good that is entirely excellent and perfect, the good that God spoke of when he created the world and called it good.

And what is good and perfect? Romans 12:2 tells us it is the will of God. "Do not be conformed to this world, but be transformed by the renewal of your mind, that by testing you may discern what is the will of God, what is good and acceptable and perfect." When we seek what is good, we seek the will of God. And when we seek the will of God, we seek what is good. That which is good is that which honors God.

Once we have determined that something is good and pleasing to God, we are to hold fast to it. This is where we so often go wrong. God opens our eyes to some new doctrine from the Bible, yet we simply shrug our shoulders and walk away. But when we hold fast, we do not grip a teaching loosely and casually; we cling to it as we might cling to the hand of a person who keeps us from falling from a cliff to the rocks below. This holding is passionate and strenuous. We are to embrace what is good and to accept it, incorporating it into what we do and believe. We rejoice that God has been gracious to reveal more of his truth to us. This is a cause for celebration! It does not matter what this thing is. If it is truly good, we must hold on to it. We may not choose to accept or reject it. We must accept it, believe it, do it, and hold fast to it.

ACTION 17: APPLY

If a doctrine or an action is shown to be biblical, write down what you will do and what truths of Scripture you will hold fast to. Alternatively, if a doctrine or an action is wrong, write down what you will substitute for it. In terms of our case study, it seems clear that God does not require me to forgive myself for my sin. Rather, I need to ask God's forgiveness and, having confessed and repented of my sin, I need to hold fast to God's promises that he has forgiven me. My primary responsibility is not to myself but to God. When I sin against another person or against myself, I primarily sin against God, and thus it is his forgiveness that I require most. I can live without the forgiveness of men; I can live without self-forgiveness.

But I cannot live without God's forgiveness. My responsibility and my privilege is to receive God's forgiveness, trusting that when I confess, "he is faithful and just to forgive us our sins and to cleanse us from all unrighteousness" (1 John 1:9).

I will substitute a God-centered approach to sin for a man-centered approach. I will hold fast to the truth that it is God who is most offended when I sin. It is God who must forgive me.

The application of these truths may be a deeply personal matter. I may need to change the way I ask God for forgiveness. I may need to extend greater effort in seeking the forgiveness of others. I may need to repent before God of taking his holiness so lightly that I could believe that my sin has been primarily against myself. In either case, I hold fast to the truths that have been revealed to me, praising God for them. I turn more fully to him and trust in the sufficiency and efficacy of his forgiveness.

The practice of discernment, then, is given to us in the Bible. We test by using God's Word as our standard. And having done that either we hold fast to what is true or abstain from what is false and substitute what is good and true and consistent with God's character for error. As we do this, God will guide us to his truth, and we will be confident that we are doing his will. We will live lives of wisdom and discernment. We will honor God.

KEY THOUGHT

We test doctrine by prayer, instinct, conscience, Scripture, and the consensus of the church. We hold up a teaching to the light of God's Word and allow him to speak to us through the Bible, revealing what is true and false. We look for points of agreement and points of departure between the teaching we are testing and the truth of the Bible. When a doctrine is false, we flee from it and substitute instead what is good. When a doctrine is true and pure, we cling to it and rejoice in it.

the DISCIPLINE of DISCERNMENT

O Timothy, guard the deposit entrusted to you.

1 TIMOTHY 6:20

IN CHAPTER 2 I wrote about David Vetter, the boy who was born with a condition that crippled his immune system. He was born with only the slimmest chance of living a long and productive life and, not surprisingly, was able to live only thirteen years. Today we hear a lot about HIV, another disease that afflicts the immune system. Unlike Vetter's illness, which never allowed him to develop an immune system, HIV cripples what was formerly a healthy and functioning immune system, steadily destroying the body's ability to resist disease by attacking a particular group of white blood cells that serve to protect the body against germs, bacteria, and viruses. As this happens, the body becomes susceptible to other opportunistic infections that are waiting to attack while defenses are weakened. The spectrum of symptoms and illnesses that can happen when HIV infection significantly depletes the body's immune defenses is called acquired immunodeficiency syndrome, or AIDS.[1] There is no cure for HIV and once it has progressed to AIDS, it is terminal.

Discernment functions as the church's immune system, pro-

---

[1] "HIV/AIDS" (http://www.intelihealth.com/IH/ihtIH/WSIHW000/9339/9419.html).

tecting the body from false teaching. When discernment is attacked and destroyed, a flood of opportunistic false teaching is waiting to attack through the weakened defenses. Nobody dies from lack of discernment or by not believing in discernment. Rather, a lack of discernment leaves people to wither under the attack of false doctrine. A lack of discernment leaves Christians unable to protect themselves and others, and allows sin to flood in. But unlike HIV, there is a cure for a lack of discernment.

God offers you this cure when he offers you spiritual discernment. Empowered by his Spirit, you can be equipped to distinguish "light from darkness, truth from error, best from better, righteousness from unrighteousness, purity from defilement, and principles from pragmatics."[2] In practicing discernment you can anticipate growing and maturing in your faith and bringing glory to God for the spiritual life he has bestowed upon you. You can heed his call to guard the precious deposit of the gospel that has been entrusted to you. You can please God and bring glory to his name if you practice the discipline of spiritual discernment.

---

[2]J. Stowell, *Fan the Flame* (Chicago: Moody, 1986), 44.

RESOURCES for DISCERNMENT

THERE ARE MANY MINISTRIES and web sites that claim to be discernment ministries. Many of these need to be approached with the utmost caution. Too many of them equate being discerning with being watchdogs, creating lists of Christian leaders and collecting examples of any indiscretion these leaders make. This is not the biblical pattern for discernment. While some good and useful information can be culled from these sites, I am hesitant to recommend any of them. I would encourage you to exercise great care and (dare I say it?) discernment with these ministries.

Please visit my web site (Challies.com) for lists of articles that present biblical wisdom on the topic of discernment and join with other Christians as we wrestle with the challenge of being discerning Christians.

Here is a short list of some of my favorite titles dealing with particular issues I have covered in this book.

BOOKS ABOUT DISCERNMENT

- Jay Adams, *A Call to Discernment* (Harvest House, 1987; out of print but available electronically or through used booksellers)
- John MacArthur, *Reckless Faith* (Crossway Books; out of print but available electronically or through used booksellers)

- John MacArthur, *Fool's Gold* (Crossway Books, 2005)
- Erwin Lutzer, *Who Are You to Judge?* (Moody, 2002)

BOOKS ABOUT THE GOSPEL

- C. J. Mahaney, *Living the Cross Centered Life* (Multnomah, 2006)
- Jerry Bridges, *The Discipline of Grace* (NavPress, 1994)

BOOKS ABOUT TRUTH

- Andreas Kostenberger, *Whatever Happened to Truth?* (Crossway, 2005)
- John MacArthur, *The Truth War* (Thomas Nelson, 2007)
- Nancy Pearcey, *Total Truth* (Crossway Books, 2004)
- Francis Schaeffer. I would suggest you begin with his trilogy of *The God Who Is There, Escape from Reason,* and *He Is There and He Is Not Silent.* These titles are available together in a single volume. (Crossway Books, 1990)
- David Wells, *No Place for Truth* (Eerdmans, 1993) This book begins a series of four titles, all of which deal with our culture's attitude toward truth.

BOOKS ABOUT GOD'S WILL

- Gary Friesen, *Decision Making and the Will of God* (Multnomah, 1980)
- Phillip Jensen and Tony Payne, *Guidance and the Voice of God* (Matthias Media, 1997)
- John MacArthur, *Found: God's Will* (Chariot Victor, 1998)
- Dave Swavely, *Decisions, Decisions* (P&R, 2003)

BOOKS ABOUT JUDGMENTALISM

- Erwin Lutzer, *Who Are You to Judge?* (Moody, 2002)
- Dave Swavely, *Who Are You to Judge?* (P&R, 2005)

BOOKS ABOUT CHRISTIAN CHARACTER AND SPIRITUAL DISCIPLINES

- Wayne Mack, *Humility: The Forgotten Virtue* (P&R, 2005)

- C. J. Mahaney, *Humility: True Greatness* (Multnomah, 2005)
- Don Whitney, *Spiritual Disciplines for the Christian Life* (NavPress, 1991)

BOOKS ABOUT STUDYING AND INTERPRETING THE BIBLE

- John MacArthur, *How to Get the Most from God's Word* (Word, 1997)
- Richard Mayhue, *How to Interpret the Bible for Yourself* (Christian Focus, 1997)
- R. C. Sproul, *Knowing Scripture* (InterVarsity, 1977)

MINISTRIES AND MISCELLANEA

- *Discerning Reader* (www.discerningreader.com). A web site I own and operate that is dedicated to providing discerning reviews of books that are of interest to Christians. There are hundreds of reviews available on a wide variety of titles.
- *MinistryWatch.* An organization that keeps tabs on ministries, sharing objective research and ratings on hundreds of churches and ministries.
- *New Attitude 2007.* This conference dealt with the topic of spiritual discernment and featured addresses by John Piper, Josh Harris, Mark Dever, Al Mohler, and other men, who were instrumental in shaping this book. Audio recordings of the keynote addresses are available at the web site (www.newattitude.org).

I'd like to make special mention of John MacArthur, as he has long stressed the importance of discernment in his ministry. His sermons, books, study Bible, and Bible commentaries are filled with references to discernment. He never seems to miss the opportunity to point out discernment as application to any passage that is relevant to the subject. If you are going to do further study of discernment, I commend his books and commentaries to you.

ACKNOWLEDGMENTS

THOUGH I HAD LONG ASSUMED that writing a book is a solo pursuit, the last year has shown this to be a false assumption. While I have spent countless hours alone in my office staring at a computer screen and tapping away on a keyboard, I have depended all the while on so many others. I'd like to take just a few lines to acknowledge these people.

God has been overwhelmingly gracious to me in writing this book. He has gone far beyond the ordinary and provided in ways I would never have expected. There have been countless memorable "God moments" along the way. If I ever doubted God's presence and assistance in writing this book, these moments reassured me and convinced me that he has been fully involved. I am exceedingly grateful, for without his presence and support I would have nothing to say. And so I'd like to first acknowledge God's gracious providence and thank him for it. I also offer special thanks to:

Crossway, the publisher of this book, for taking a chance on this first-time author. I am grateful for the opportunity and hope to work with you again very soon. I offer special gratitude to my editor (and new friend) Lydia Brownback for your patience in trying to help me make the difficult transition from a writer to an author.

Justin Taylor and Joshua Harris—two godly men the Lord used to convince me to begin this writing project. I am grateful for your friendship and your encouragement. I still think Josh should have written this book.

All of those who have made my blog (challies.com) a part of their lives. Without the interest in that web site, this book would not have come about. I have enjoyed getting to know many of you either face-to-face or online. I am indebted to you for your support, your input, and your prayers. As you no doubt realized, there were several occasions on which I used you as a testing ground for my ideas. I know this book is better because of your feedback.

Those friends who suffered through reading this manuscript while it was still coming together and while it was still very rough. Thanks to David, Justin, Jeri, Trevin, Aileen, Annette, Paul, Peter, Katherine, Adrian, and Barbara (a.k.a. Mom). All of you provided indispensable advice. Special thanks to Mark Dever for several timely suggestions. In fact, with the quantity and quality of people who read this book, I should surely be absolved of any blame for problems that remain.

My church family at Grace Fellowship Church (gfcto.com), and in particular to our pastor, Paul Martin, for being a theological consultant, for lending me any books and commentaries I needed, and for writing a really awful poem in honor of this book's completion. I am grateful to have found a faithful church that cares so much about serving God through those extraordinarily beautiful, ordinary means of grace. I love to worship, pray, and learn with all of you so that we together can delight in God to the glory of God.

My family: Mom and Dad for raising me to know and love the Lord, and my brother and sisters for loving and supporting me. There's still lots of room in Canada if any of you ever want to move back.

Nicholas, Abigail, and Michaela for love and laughs and for heeding the many admonitions to "be quiet please! Daddy's working on his book."

My beautiful Aileen. You continually become more precious to me, and I look forward to a lifetime of getting to know you better. God was good to provide me with such a loving, attentive, godly wife.

STUDY GUIDE

STUDY QUESTIONS FOR CHAPTER 1

1) Read Solomon's prayer in 1 Kings 3:6–9 and jot down a few of the ways in which you have been called to exercise leadership.

2) As you consider the areas in which you have to exercise leadership, do you feel adequate to the task? Why or why not?

3) Do you consider *discernment* a word with positive or negative connotations?

4) How would you define *discernment*?

5) Do you consider yourself a spiritually discerning person? Are you discerning in other aspects of life?

6) Of all the people you have met, who is the one with the greatest spiritual discernment? What evidence of discernment have you seen from this person?

7) Summarize the three marks of discernment and the three marks of a lack of discernment.

8) Do you see evidence of spiritual life within yourself? What might this say about you?

9) Do you see evidence of spiritual growth in your life? What might this say about you?

10) Do you see evidence of increasing spiritual maturity? What might this say about you?

STUDY QUESTIONS FOR CHAPTER 2

1) In your experience, is spiritual discernment a trait that is likely to make a person popular or unpopular within the church? Why?

2) Describe the three broad categories of influences you should expect to see arrayed against you as you seek to be a person of discernment.

3) Can you think of a time that your own sinfulness kept you from exercising discernment?

4) What are some concrete ways that the full armor of God can protect you against the spiritual influences that seek to keep you from growing in discernment?

5) Which of the four cultural influences in this chapter do you feel most seriously impacts your ability to be discerning?

6) Can you think of other cultural influences that inhibit spiritual discernment?

STUDY QUESTIONS FOR CHAPTER 3

1) Think back to your definition of discernment as you defined it in chapter 1. Was your definition similar to the one introduced in this chapter? What was the same? What was different?

2) We learn from the structure of the book of Proverbs that God deals with character before he deals with conduct. What are some areas where God may need to address your character before he can address your conduct?

3) Define wisdom. How do wisdom and discernment differ? How are they related?

4) Describe the key terms that arise from a study of the word *discernment* in the original languages.

5) What is the end, or ultimate goal, of discernment?

6) "Discernment begins and ends with God." What does this mean? How can you apply this in your life?

STUDY QUESTIONS FOR CHAPTER 4

1) When you are handed money do you test it to ensure it is genuine? Why or why not? Are you confident that you would know counterfeit money from genuine money?

2) First Thessalonians 5:21 tells us to "test everything." What are some synonyms for "test?"

3) Take a look at the list of first-order doctrines. Are there any of these you struggle with? Are there any you are unsure of? If so, what are you going to do about it?

4) How are we to react to those who claim to be Christian but deny the first-order doctrines?

5) Under the category of second-order doctrine, I listed the ongoing, miraculous gifts of the Holy Spirit and the mode and meaning of baptism. What are some other examples of second-order doctrine?

6) How are we to react to Christians with whom we disagree about second-order doctrines? What things could we do with these people and what things would we need to avoid?

7) Under the category of third-order doctrine, I listed beliefs about the end times. What are some other third-order doctrines you can think of that may be held by people within your local church?

8) What do the Scriptures principally teach? Said otherwise, what are the two main thrusts of the Bible's teaching?

9) What are the two broad areas in which we need to practice discernment? In which of these do you feel most confident in your ability to be discerning?

STUDY QUESTIONS FOR CHAPTER 5

1) Define *truth*.

2) Francis Schaeffer wrote, "On the basis of the Scriptures, while we do not have exhaustive knowledge, we have true and unified knowledge." Why is it so important that we understand the notion of total truth.

3) Why is it so important that we think rightly about God?

4) What is worldliness? What are some words or phrases that may be associated with worldliness?

5) What is the one defining characteristic of doctrine that is false?

6) Why is it important that we focus our primary efforts in discernment on studying truth rather than error?

7) Can you think of some "gray areas" you have encountered in your efforts at discernment? How did you react to them?

STUDY QUESTIONS FOR CHAPTER 6

1) What is God's secret will?

2) What is God's revealed will?

3) Why is it important that we learn to distinguish between God's secret will and his revealed will?

4) Does discernment deal primarily with God's secret will or with his revealed will? How do we know?

5) Can we ever be outside the will of God?

6) How do we know that we are truly becoming discerning in knowing and obeying God's will?

STUDY QUESTIONS FOR CHAPTER 7

1) Does your local church emphasize the spiritual gifts and provide opportunities to practice them?

2) Have you ever asked your friends or church leaders how you have been gifted by the Spirit? If you answered no, why haven't you?

3) If you have asked your friends and church leaders how you have been gifted by the Spirit, what did they tell you? How have you acted on it?

4) How do you feel you have been gifted by the Spirit? How do you practice this gifting?

5) What are the two closely related purposes of spiritual gifts?

6) Whom do you know who may have the gift of spiritual discernment?

7) What are some ways that people with the gift of discernment may be able to exercise the gift in your local church?

STUDY QUESTIONS FOR CHAPTER 8

1) What does the Bible mean when it says we are to "be wise as to what is good and innocent as to what is evil?" Would your friends and family say this admonition is true of you?

2) How can it be spiritually damaging to give undue attention to what is evil?

3) Why is it so easy for something good, such as discernment, to be used for evil?

4) Describe the eight dangers of discernment listed in this chapter. Are there other dangers you would add to this list?

5) Which of the eight dangers do you struggle with most?

6) Why are pure motives so important in our pursuit and practice of discernment?

STUDY QUESTIONS FOR CHAPTER 9

1) Why is it that the pursuit of spiritual discernment cannot be isolated from other disciplines of the Christian life?

2) What four commitments are necessary for Christians who wish to be discerning? Which of these do you struggle with? Why?

3) What role does the local church play in the pursuit and practice of discernment?

4) In what ways does the pursuit of discernment depend upon humility before God? Or, said otherwise, how can spiritual arrogance make discernment an impossible pursuit?

5) In what ways does the pursuit of discernment depend upon humility before other believers? How can independence and arrogance handicap the Christian's ability to be discerning?

6) Can a person who knows right from wrong and good from evil but refuses to put this knowledge into practice be considered discerning? Why or why not?

7) What proof of discernment do you see in your life?

STUDY QUESTIONS FOR CHAPTER 10

1) Why is it important that we properly prepare before beginning the process of discernment?

2) What are the five steps of testing a doctrine? Which of these are easiest for you? Which give you the most difficulty?

3) What does it mean to hold a teaching up to the light?

4) What is the importance of looking for points of agreement?

5) What is the importance of looking for points of departure?

6) We are to abstain from every form of evil. What are some synonyms for *abstain*?

7) Why is the principle of substitution important when we abstain from a false teaching?

8) Why is it so important that we hold fast to what is good?

9) Do you struggle with embracing and celebrating the true and good things God has revealed to you through his Word? If so, how?

GENERAL INDEX

SCRIPTURE INDEX